Queer Astrology Anthology
Presentations from the Queer Astrology Conference
July 20-21, 2013

Edited by Ian Waisler & Rhea Wolf

Contributors: Erica Jones, Jessica Lanyadoo, Gary Lorentzen, Barry Perlman,
Christopher Renstrom, Ian Waisler, Rhea Wolf,
and Queer Astrology Conference Panel

© 2014, Queer Astrology
San Francisco, CA

Copyright © 2014 by Queer Astrology

This book or any portion thereof may be reproduced or used in manners consistent with the Creative Commons standards of sharing in order to create a culture of free access to our shared knowledge. To republish any article in its entirety, please contact the author of that article.

Printed ISBN: 978-0-9960567-0-0
E-Book ISBN: 978-0-9960567-1-7

Queer Astrology
San Francisco, CA

For more information visit queerastrology.com

Dedicated to the memory of Jack Fertig,
and to all the ancestor astrologers,
queer ones and others who worked
tirelessly and sometimes invisibly
to bring illumination and love to the world.

Contents

Acknowledgments vii

Foreword ~ Gary Lorentzen ix

Why a Queer Astrology? ~ Ian Waisler 3

Toward a Queer Astrology ~ Opening Panel 9

The Saturn Return of AIDS ~ Christopher Renstrom 27

Myths of Gender, Gender in Myth ~ Rhea Wolf 65

Queer Talk on Client Work ~ Barry Perlman and Jessica Lanyadoo 75

Ecosexuality: Liberating the Venus Within Pluto ~ Erica Jones 99

Contributors 119

Acknowledgments

THE Queer Astrology Anthology and the 2013 Conference which it documents was a labor of love offered by more hands and hearts than can be named here. Foremost I'd like to acknowledge Stella "The Good Witch" Lawson whose unwavering support through the months of birthing the event itself cannot be expressed in words. Likewise Rhea Wolf without whose collaboration the project of bringing this book to life might never have been realized. My appreciation for both your time and care is as endless as the stars.

For their roles in Queer Astrology's gestation phases, I honor Chani Nicholas, Barry Perlman, Clare Martin, and the subtle nudge of Christopher Renstrom. For stellar contributions in planning the conference I thank dearly Erin D'Estrée, Tino Calenda, Stephanie Gailing, Laurence Jones, Luciano Sagastume, and Marc Matheson. And of course the presenters not already named: Yolo Akili, Eric Francis Coppolino, Diego Fitzgerald, Erica Jones, Jessica Lanyadoo, Lilia Leshan, and Rod O'Neal.

Organizational support came powerfully from the Sisters of Perpetual Indulgence, especially Sisters Merry Peter and Barbra Ganesh. The San Francisco Astrological Society backed the project as well, with dedicated contributions from Linea Van Horn, Nora Jean Stone, and Philip Witkay. And of course Jack Fertig, our elder astrologer and activist, whose memorial anchored the event and serves to remind us how our work always rests on the bones of our ancestors.

At CIIS, special thanks to Lauren Selfridge, Shirley Strong, Lisa Sowunmi, and Craig Chalquist whose support gave the event a home, as well as so many others who maintain that academy of edge-pushing scholarship, and tend it as one of the few places where astrology is studied in the US. For video archiving Mark McBeth, Kay O. Sweaver, and Astral Projection Film Works. For donations to our fundraising campaign, Joolie Geldner, Krista Herbe, Michelle Tea, Annabelle Drda, Stargazer Li, Demetrius Bagley, Luette, and Ray Himmelman.

In production of this book, volunteer transcriptionists Willow Aevery, Wonder Bright, Amanda Moreno, and Shawn Nygaard were all so generous with their time. And finally Corina Dross, Gary Lorentzen, Phyllis Wipf, and Barry Perlman for editing our so many voices into the polished form you have before you.

Thank you to everyone who cared or contributed in so many seen and unseen ways. And dear reader, thanks to you for giving all our work its reason for being.

Foreword

Gary Lorentzen

It has been a year now since the first Queer Astrology Conference took place in San Francisco and it is perhaps time to reflect on what happened there, how it came to be and where it will lead us into the future. There was an initial gathering of interested astrologers last spring in San Francisco, whose discussions and idea-sharing led to the planning of the summer conference. There was surprise expressed by many that there had not been a Queer Astrology Conference before 2013. After all, academic studies in Queer theory and Feminist theory have been part of mainstream intellectual efforts for more than thirty years now, and gays and feminists long ago found a kinship with astrology and astrological studies. So, why was there this cultural lag within the astrological community that has taken so long to bring Queerness and Feminism into mainstream astrological inquiry and criticism, at least to the degree that there could be a Queer Astrology Conference in 2013?

A thorough answer to that question is probably more complicated than what can be outlined in a foreword to these transcripts of last year's Queer Astrology Conference. There probably needs to be a serious academic study of the history of feminists, gay people and their contributions to the field of astrology. However, there are rather common-sense suggestions for possible answers to the question based on the remembrances and insights of those older astrologers who began moving astrology in a new, humanistic direction in the late 1960s and 1970s, and who knew very well most of the gay and queer astrologers of the period. To that end, my conversations with Donna Cunningham, Alan Oken, Diana Stone, and Erin Sullivan helped me remember some of the queer and feminist astrologers who shaped the study and discipline of astrological practice. They reminded me that the struggle for civil rights, women's rights and gay rights of that period opened up the previous astrological community to hippies, a new generation of intellectual and well-educated astrologers, Blacks, young Feminists and Gay men. This new generation of astrologers began integrating their life-experiences and their education into astrological practice, and as a result, new astrological theories and ideas began influencing the world of astrology. New concepts like Marc Robertson's "Cosmopsychology" and Michael Meyer's "Humanistic Astrology," the influence of classical mythology and archetypes presented by Joseph Campbell and Carl Jung in re-interpreting planets and their roles in human behavior, as well as the continued work in depth psychology originally introduced by Dane Rudhyar in the 1930s (*The Astrology of Personality*) and promoted and further developed by Liz Greene, Howard Sasportas, et al, all served to bring a new astrological culture and a new body of literature into being. Part of this period of innovation included a large number of gay men and women who proved to be a driving force behind this new humanistic approach to astrology.

In spite of the queer and feminist influence in the new humanistic approaches, being openly gay was still problematic in astrological circles in the 1970s and 1980s. In spite of the very nature of astrology, most students and practitioners were not that open to knowing who was queer, much less having open discussions about it. Initially, all of the queer astrologers stayed quite closeted. This was reflected in the society at large, but when the AIDS epidemic began, it decimated the ranks of our gay astrologers. No fewer than fifteen gay professionals died during the epidemic and the initial impetus for a Queer Astrology died with them. Millions died across the country and queer people began to get angry at the lack of response and the general prejudice and ignorance. It became necessary to act up and act out–and that meant change the culture to accept coming out as a part of the queer experience. This also began to happen in the astrological community. Gay astrologers began outing themselves, because it was clear that silence meant death. Open discussion, recognition and honest discourse were the goals for those of us who were still alive. Although things began changing in the country and around the world, within astrological circles coming out didn't seem to make much of an impact. In the final analysis, we had simply lost too many of our most important queer astrologers to AIDS and there just weren't enough voices left to bring the message home.

That does not change the fact that many gay men were behind the humanistic and psychological approaches to astrological interpretation and they were, in fact, the first phases of what we would now call the "queering" of astrology. However, once we lost so many of our great astrologers in the '80s-90s, we also lost the momentum in developing a body of openly queer literature, theory and criticism. Without their presence, inspiration and charisma, queerness in astrology simply languished. The global astrological community simply did not evolve any further in its understanding of queer people and their lives.

Interpretations of the birth chart most often reflected the archaic, pathological view of queer sexuality as inverted, perverted, confused or simply willful rebellion. Astrologers were still telling people that their sexual identity could be found in the birth chart. Both gay astrologers and gay clientele were still being alienated by those so-called experts who had such answers for them. In fact, many astrologers still believe and maintain that they can find homosexuality in the birth chart. This fact alone makes it clear that the process of queering astrology is not complete—we still have hard work ahead of us. However, there is now a new generation of astrologers that has been influenced by Queer and Feminist theory, and they are part of a larger cultural shift that includes and integrates queer and gay people into our mainstream, everyday life. They are open-minded, filled with empathy and new life and intellectual experiences that are beginning to change astrological attitudes, culture and practice, just as my generation did back in the 1970s. They have made it a goal in this postmodern world to deconstruct astrological interpretation and practice and renovate it with queer and feminist theory and criticism. They have begun anew where the older generations' queer and gay astrologers and their efforts left off.

The Queer Astrology Conference of 2013 was a first step in bringing these new efforts into focus. Their influence is beginning to be felt at mainstream conferences where even the older generation has begun talking about sexuality and relationships in a new light that is colored somewhat queerly. So I applaud and encourage their efforts here to continue the work that was begun decades ago, work that was influenced by queer and feminist theory, but that unfortunately was left incomplete after the tragic impact of AIDS in our astrological community. The challenge is to develop a new body of astrological literature that will reflect what has happened here and now, as well as fulfill the dream of the previous generation of queer astrologers. This current movement to queer astrology, to organize conferences, and to create a new mode of interpretation must result in the publication of these ideas in our collective body of astrological work. This book is clearly a first effort in creating our future and an excellent start in educating our colleagues as to the nature of the vision.

~ Gary Lorentzen
June 30, 2014

Queer Astrology Anthology

Why a Queer Astrology?

Ian Waisler

THE question of how to, or even whether to, recognize queer people is emerging in the mass consciousness. Queer indicates broadly anyone who does not conform to traditional patterns and norms. By many accounts, the place of gays, lesbians, bisexual and transgendered individuals has never been so free and equal, and without a doubt the LGBT community is currently enjoying unprecedented visibility and access in (some) parts of the world. At the same time, efforts to exclude and to divide populations along these lines have succeeded in some countries. Even a cursory glance around the globe reveals that queer people are still struggling and our issues are far from settled.

The potential violence and hardship that results from ignoring these issues cannot be underestimated. Families divide and cast out their own, just as political and religious bodies shun and curse those they are pledged to serve. Most achingly, queer individuals are too often split not only from our environments, but within ourselves.

The astrological community tends to focus on its own strengths of technique and its living history. We emphasize our basic concerns of health and well-being and our common needs of hope and joy. Astrologers debate points of practice, but for the most part, self-inquiry around how we as astrologers uphold or confront cultural norms tends to fall to the background. And who could blame us for trying to stick together, when in the eyes of so many self-validating outside critics, astrology is the "gold standard of superstition?"[1]

Too many astrological lectures and literature reflect the norms taken for granted by a reductionist mainstream culture. Straight lives are not just perceived as the norm, heterosexuality is often portrayed as the only healthy sexuality, and others are at best ignored and at worst simply declared pathological. Yet perhaps this is too harsh a criticism, for even 50 years ago these queer concerns were so fully constrained by the culture, it was, where not illegal, socially impossible to bring any light to them.

---

1. Tarnas, Rick. "The Role of Astrology in a Civilization in Crisis." Astrological Association of Great Britain Conference, 28 September 2013.

It is in this profound imbalance and injustice that we are called to this work to make our visibility a part of a much greater remedy. Astrologers are a relatively small population who would do well to stick together. So as we bring forth some points of view of queer-identified people working in astrology, we invite our colleagues to incorporate our queries as our shared common tradition evolves. Our understandings of health and well-being, hope and joy may yet open and transform astrological thought, practice and literature through an encounter with otherness. Queer Astrology calls us all to come out.

* * *

The tribe at the heart of this project, all of us with Pluto in tropical Libra, met at the 2012 United Astrology Conference in New Orleans. Within this huge convocation, we found essentially no mention of homosexuality, much less any indication of queerness, in the at-large discourse. We felt an invitation to action. These categories of otherness were handily relegated to being beyond the scope of what might bring astrologers together. Classical and modern traditions of gender, assumptions around sex and marriage, and an absence of reference to patriarchy, whiteness, capitalism, and colonialism begged attention.

In the autumn after UAC, there was talk within the San Francisco Astrological Society around organizing an event to honor Jack Fertig, a much beloved activist and organizer both in astrology and gay liberation. With his memory and bright spirit as a guide, the spark of an event took root.

Meanwhile in the skies, the Uranus-Pluto squares continued to apply. It will not surprise anyone that under these transits some of us were moved to register certain as-of-yet unarticulated points of view. The urgency of the moment buoyed our efforts and inspired boldness and risk-taking. We began to gather in pursuit of a queer astrology, curious whether our experiment would find an audience and whether these perspectives might offer something—to our colleagues and peers, to our history and our future—which had been missing.

While the meme Queer Astrology had immediate traction, it is also worthwhile to acknowledge the edges of its reach. One promoter reported a client of hers, a lesbian woman in her 80s, could not conceive of going anywhere near a *queer* conference. Another professional astrologer begged my pause, admitting she could not focus on what I was saying; she was quite thrown at hearing me call myself and the work I had been doing *queer*.

To some of you, these cases will land as extremes or outliers which do not speak to the central thrust of the project one imagines as queering astrology, but they speak significantly to our context. This Queer Astrology project is dedicated to sharing the wisdom of our queer lives with our peers and elders who have had no points of entry to these experiences. And at the same time, it's intended to provide upcoming generations an opportunity to find themselves plainly on the page instead of between the lines, where many of us have had to look for ourselves.

Some of the aims of this work are to locate our lives in our astrology and to share their fruit with others who'll benefit from our experiences. We are curious how common technique and theory may evolve given our contributions. The work is not limited specifically to concerns of sexuality, central though those may be in our lives. But in the tradition of queers and theorists, Queer Astrology seeks to interrogate all the assumptions in our symbols and open further interpretative turns available to us. What if our received wisdom no longer comes from cultures which prize domination and which are blind to their own privilege? What if our techniques seek not to stabilize in sameness, but rather orient toward and embrace difference?

* * *

Organized in the span of about six months, the first Queer Astrology Conference was held July 20 and 21, 2013, at the California Institute of Integral Studies in San Francisco. The call went out as follows:

> *We call professional and novice astrologers to come together to explore the intersections of study/practice and queer-identified life. By queer, we invite a broadly imagined array of gender and sexual diversity, self-defined identities and lived experiences.*
>
> *The intent is to work smarter in the present and to generate queer-specific resources for future astrologers. Through sharing audio, video and written record of the proceedings, we hope to further the research, scholarship, and practice of astrology relevant to ourselves as queer people.*

Grounded in our lived experience as queer people, we came together to add upon our too few representations in the astrological literature and practice. Presentations touched on our theory and practice through lenses of sexuality, religion, politics, history, mysticism, feminism, and myth, among others. Caucus spaces were convened to hold discussions among attendees who identified as transgender, genderqueer, and people-of-color, as well as cisgender and white allies. The obvious intersections of these points of inquiry in our individual lives and their relevance to the furthering of astrology as a human language was woven into a tangible community and evoked a clear call to carry on this work. At the closing ceremony, one conference participant spoke something to the effect of, "I don't know if I've ever been in a space with so many people sharing so many of my interests, gathering to enter into all of them so consciously."

<u>Saturday</u>
What's a Queer Astrology Opening Panel
The Compatibility Myth: Queering the Astrological Lens
Astro Drag
Eco-Sexuality: Liberating the Venus in Pluto
Lilith and Adam: Gender, Sexuality and Deviance
The Saturn Return of AIDS
People of Color Caucus
White Allies Caucus
Tribute to Jack Fertig

<u>Sunday</u>
Queer Talk on Client Work
Queer Liberation and the Stars
Asteroids for Beginners: Toward a Queer Feminist Astrology
Gender in Myths, Myths of Gender
Queer Water, Queer Body, Queer Space
Holistic Sexuality and Astrology
Trans / Genderqueer Caucus
Cisgender Allies Caucus

Of course these by no means intend to represent the whole of what Queer Astrology could invoke. Yet we have each come out, over and over again. And we accept and mark ourselves as distinct and more complex and creative than any flattened cookbook interpretation or identity category can convey. Bolstered by our process of individuation, we carry the liberating wisdom of this process as essential. We have moved out from under the pressure of an ill-fitting externalized Saturn, and channeled the jolt of Promethean/Uranian breakthrough to express ourselves beyond what had been deemed possible.

* * *

This text includes a selection of documents from the conference. We have attempted to capture the spontaneity of the live event while producing a highly readable text.

First is a transcription of the opening panel, convened to lay the foundation for what this group of astrologers believed themselves to be doing together one sunny Saturday in San Francisco. It begins to map the issues and orientations which were further illuminated through the weekend.

Christopher Renstrom's work on the Saturn Return of AIDS brings together the historical and mythic dimensions of recent history, sharing an intimate take on his own search for meaning.

Rhea Wolf guides us through an exploration of returning to the gendered norms so often repeated in astrology and opening upon them with fresh, patient uncertainty and a commitment to encountering wholeness.

Jessica Lanyadoo and Barry Perlman share how their consulting practices have been shaped by years of work with a strongly queer-identified client base.

Finally Erica Jones engages us in both academic and devotional frameworks, calling on established research and theory to make connections between the personal and ecological.

These articles are offered in the full light of all the struggles and accomplishments which predate them and shape their journey to you, along with prayers that the healing and connection of our shared experiences be more easily found in years to come.

- Ian Waisler
April 2014

Toward a Queer Astrology

Opening Panel Discussion
July 20, 2013

GOOD morning, and welcome to the first ever Queer Astrology Conference. (*Audience cheers and claps enthusiastically.*) My name is Ian Waisler and I'm really tickled to see all of you here, and also aware of all of the people who are yet on their way in to join this conversation.

So something that happened a lot over the last few months was that people would ask "What is Queer Astrology? How do you practice Queer Astrology? Is there a special way of teaching it? And what really is it?" And my answer was always unsatisfying for people because I'd say "I don't know what it is" and "We're eager to explore what it is."

For the opening of the conference, I wanted to gather all the presenters and caucus facilitators who heard the call to come to this conference to introduce themselves and to talk about this. What about the idea of a Queer Astrology conference brought them here? We'll begin with Chani Nicholas.

Chani: Hi. My name is Chani. A couple of us, Barry and Ian, and other folks were at UAC last year, a big astrology conference, and we loved it and it was amazing. But we also said, "What about us? What about our voices? What about putting our lives into astrology?" And so thus began this conversation, which we felt was really important, and it's evolving and we'll see what it turns out to be this weekend. I'm just happy to be here and be with everybody. I will be giving a talk about Lilith, the story of Lilith and Adam, gender, sex and deviance, and other stuff like that.

Jessica: Hi, I'm nervous about this. OK, I'm Jessica Lanyadoo and my feeling of why I was called to do this is I've been working professionally as an astrologer for about 18 years, and for 18 years I've been working with queer folks, artists, social workers, people who kind of fall outside of the heteronormative heterotypical kind of conventional paradigms. But also with people who are wicked conventional.

I feel this conference really is a forum to address that aspect of my work, which is what the wonderful Barry and I are going to be speaking about tomorrow. I feel like this is just a really exciting opening for astrology, and for the conversation around astrology, but also societally. I think being able to acknowledge more parts of our humanity is something that's happening within astrology and outside astrology, so I'm excited to be part of that conversation and I'm excited to hear what happens.

Barry: Hello, everyone. I'm Barry Perlman. Some people know me as AstroBarry. I feel really strongly that I wanted to be involved in this. I am like many people a self-taught astrologer which means that when I found astrology I just started reading every book I could get my hands on. And of course, I started learning astrology because I was interested in myself and my chart and wanted to read the books to figure out more about myself. And like many self-taught astrologers of the queer bent, I discovered as I was reading the literature that really a lot of what was written didn't talk about me or my experiences at all.

I think queers in general are used to looking at a mainstream writing or media and finding the cracks in between it where our experiences are not discussed, and then finding ways to insert ourselves into the story. So, thankfully, I am confident enough to know how to insert myself into a story in which I am not naturally included.

But as I began doing my client work I realized that the clients of all different persuasions, who were coming to see me, also had a lot of stories that narrated their real lives, their day-to-day lives, that weren't addressed by what was written in 99.9 percent of astrology texts. And at conferences, like Chani was saying, there were no presentations that discussed these ideas whether it be queerness, transgender, or non-traditional relationship structures. And so it just seems time that those of us who actually have practical, professional experience having these conversations begin to insert ourselves into the canon of texts and conferences, so that other people like us can have their voices heard too. So I thought this was really important work to do.

Rhea: I'm Rhea Wolf and I agree with everything Barry said. (*Loud laughter as she pretends to pass the mic.*) That was just really eloquently stated, thank you.

I'm really excited to be here, and I am a little bit astounded that this *is* the first ever queer astrology conference, right? It's totally crazy, but it must be just the right time for it to happen. I feel so blessed to be here, and what draws me to this work is, as a feminist, as a witch, as somebody who also finds the more conventional way of describing experiences to be lacking. And I love the way that you put it, about finding the cracks in something and finding your way into a system through that.

I'm really interested in systems in general and how they can be helpful and then how they can be limiting. As an astrologer, I'm interested in looking and finding the whole person, the unique experience within that, and in this really tricky dance, going beyond the way that a certain planet or sign or aspect has been described for, you know, decades or thousands of years even, and asking: "Well, but what is it now? What is it in this person?"

My talk is going to be on how we can use mythology and stories, storytelling, stories of divine beings and stories from literature in order to create a queer understanding of certain planets, especially those that have been typically associated with male-gender, female-gender—and classified strictly in those ways; how we can use mythology to expand our concept of those planets and create more fluid definitions for them, definitions specific to each person. How do we bring the big into the small, I guess would be another way of describing that, the Cosmic into the Moment of an individual. Yes, yay!

Rod: Hi. I'm Rod O'Neal. And I jumped at the chance to join this when Erica Jones threw my name in the ring. I got my PhD here at CIIS with Rick Tarnas, and I'm really focused on history and mundane astrology in a lot of ways. But I do client work. I have been an astrologer for sixteen or seventeen years now.

In 2008, my dissertation was actually about the Puritan Movement, and I showed a really detailed case study that correlated with the astrological cycles really strongly. And the nature of it also was very much like its birth chart. I finished in 2008 and then Prop 8 happened and I was involved in a gay church—MCC, a queer church—and I wanted to show them that there was hope. So I dove into the astrology of the queer liberation impulses, and what I discovered that year doing that research, and the three years since then preparing lectures about it, is an astounding correlation of queer liberation impulses with the Uranus-Pluto alignments and Jupiter-Uranus alignments. We're in the middle of both of those right now, so I think it is perfect timing that we are doing this right now.

And I, like Barry and Rhea and others, when I first studied astrology, thought, "Wow, archetypes, gender defined, wow. Where's the queer person? Where's the transvestite person? Where's the transsexual person in all this?" So I'm really happy to be here. Thank you.

Erica: Hi I'm Erica Jones and I came to astrology around 2006 through the work of Richard Tarnas. I received a Master's Degree here at CIIS in the Philosophy, Cosmology, and Consciousness program. I come from an ecological perspective and regard astrology as an eco-psychology. It includes the greater-than-human world and human psyche and it embeds humanity in a larger matrix of being. I observe that unity reflects diversity; it doesn't reflect homogeneity, which means everything is the same. The earth community flourishes with diversity and celebrates this.

I feel that we humans are in a great crisis now with industrialization and our relationship to the planet, to each other and the way that industrial cultures are caught up in the trance of technological progress. The technology related to social media, for example, has created a very poor substitute for the intimacy, the belonging, the meaning and purpose that we all seek. And the human soul craves this. So I believe that one of the antidotes to this crisis of meaning is to break out of this conceptual trance around who and what a human being is.

In my practice of astrology I wish to assist people in that revolutionary act of becoming more fully human–to help people see more deeply the truth and the beauty at the center of their being–that who and what they are is outside the social concepts of what a man or woman is. And so for me the ultimate queerness is not to be a cog in the machine, or to live out the preconceived notion of what a human is, or how to love, or whom to love, and how we should carry our archetypal makeup.

All the woundedness of patriarchy and technology to me is a crisis of the ability to relate, and queer astrology is to me an act of radical love of humanity. Trusting the intelligence within each of us, and listening to that, and assisting self-determination, for I am sure it is going to bring cultural healing and wholing to the planet, to be in touch with one's deepest longing. And to be in touch with one's desire, to bring forth the unique gifts of each person, I believe, is what is going to bring forth the intimacy, the caring, and connection that our earth community needs so desperately right now, for our own humanity, and so…that's what I think. (*Loud cheering*) My talk is on ecosexuality, liberating the Venus within Pluto. Thank you.

Christopher: My name is Christopher Renstrom. This is a big day for me. I started practicing astrology at the height of the AIDS epidemic in the mid '80s, and my clientele was not exclusively people battling with HIV, it was across the board. But my experience of working with people dealing with HIV shaped everything I am today as an astrologer. Being bedside at the hospices, being with friends, being with family, starting as an astrologer, I think it stripped away what could potentially have been bad astrology habits: putting everything in the prediction, putting everything in the technique, putting everything into explaining the karmic reason why this was happening.

All of those things disappeared immediately, and to look at a chart in which the future was not—in 1985, '86, '87, '88, '89, and it goes on, you know–it was not particularly bright. What do you do when you're *with* someone? And so it taught me to read, to read the chart, not to have the answer, not to come up with this or that or whatever, but to read the chart, to tell the story of the chart, and in turn, to tell the story of the person, who was looking for that.

I don't know if I'm doing the best job of describing that, but that really shaped me as an astrologer and gave me such a great love of this art form, a faith in a time of faithlessness, when there was just nothing to really hold on to. But there was the chart, there were the planets, there were these signs. So for me, as I said, that not only shaped me obviously as a gay man, but also as an astrologer.

And through our history and our culture and those experiences I feel it really gave me a very unique way of practicing the art form. That's always potentially there, it's there for anyone, but it taught me that art, that art of reading, not to predict, not to say what this is about, but just to be there with the person and with the chart and with the art form.

So my talk is on the Saturn Return of AIDS, and what does that mean for a pandemic, what did it do, what does it do, and what would be the questions we would ask of that? So, that's that.

Luciano: Hi, I'm Luciano. I just wanted to say, everyone said such amazing things up here, I'm just really blown away. I've been thinking a lot about queer astrology. When Ian asked me to write something, I felt really strongly that one of the greatest gifts that I've gotten from astrology has been to just really, as you were saying, to just value the chart and the person, and find ways to help people move past what is expected of us, in this heteronormative patriarchal culture that oppresses a lot of us, and forces us into certain movements or places that don't value all of what is in somebody's chart, or the different ways that they can be.

And I find it really powerful to just *be* who you are and let astrology open up people to different experiences. And so for me it's really important for the writing of astrology to reflect that and to open it up and separate it from heteronormativity, patriarchy, normalizing forces, and really let people explore their chart in new ways and find new meanings for what these planets have been and could be in the future, if we just start living them, fully, in the moment. I think that that's what it means to me.

I just want to say one more time, I was talking about this earlier and I just didn't know what to say. And Diego and I were talking about how we just wanted to mention patriarchy (*Laughter*). I was just so glad every time somebody's mentioned it, I've been like (*Ominous voice*) patriarchy. (*Loud laughter*)

Rhea: It would be great if we could have an echo ... *patriarchy*.

Diego: My name is Diego. Queer astrology. It's been said so many times already, so I'm just going to say that reading charts for me is important because it reminds me that everybody has a place in the world and has work to do in the world. Queer Astrology is important because it reminds me that it is important to come together and remind each other of that fact, and to work together with each other. So that's it. Luciano and I are doing the POC caucus and the trans caucus.

Laurence: Now that the awkward black guy has the microphone, yay. (*Laughter*) My name is Laurence Jones. And that is my mom back there. (*Clapping*) So, I was trying to calculate what I was going to say in my head as everybody else was talking, and here I go.

I'm probably one of the people who is a little bit newer to astrology, or my knowledge isn't as deep, and as I've learned, more of the texts reflect to me the negative or positive without realizing or expressing that there's an energy pull, a dynamic interaction, between negative and positive. And that those words, positive and negative, are really horrible words even to define astrology or define what we are looking for in astrology. So for me it is more about being in a community that actually speaks a language that I feel comfortable with, and that I find more positive and affirming, and beneficial, instead of something like, unfortunately, the ways that organized religion has traipsed its way into astrology and defined it in a way that is very Western, Christian, and very patriarchal (*Echo in the crowd of people repeating the word patriarchal. Laughter.*) There we go! Third time's the charm, get it out there.

So establishing something new and being on the ground floor in a community that's redefining its methods, and looking at how to integrate all walks of life, all types of people and all types of narratives in the human story is why I'm here. So as I learn, I want to express a far more positive, holistic way of looking at astrology and how it reflects everybody's lives. I will be with Chani co-facilitating the Cisgender Allies Caucus.

Ian: Something that I would have done before if I had more wherewithal was invite everyone to take a few breaths together. (*Crowd takes a few breaths together*)

Alongside of how much we learn astrology in books, my interest is really in what astrology means given that we have bodies and are not just words. I really wanted to be here and in this university to encourage us all to not feel like we need to play the same role that we were taught around the Teacher and the Student, or The Idea versus The Experience. Things that echo what has been said: to try and pull the archetypes into the body a little more and get to know them.

What else wants to be said here? To go further with that, queer is something that most of us—no, all right, no generalizations—*I* found that queer was something I found in my body, and there was this self-knowing that led to a coming out. And not *the* coming out but even as I talk to people about coming out, for many of us who sit here this is yet another coming out, to sit in front of the room and to be willing to go on record and talk and show up. And I want to just send that around the room that everyone gets the chance to keep coming out through this work. That's my wish and blessing.

I'm going to talk tomorrow around the chart of the day, the chart of the week, the chart of the year, and locate what we're doing in the specific symbols. It's called Queer Water, Queer Body, Queer Space. Thank you.

Stella: Wow, it's beautiful to see all your faces. I really encourage everybody to look around and take in who's here. I feel so much gratitude that this labor of love is finally happening. I just want to start off by naming that we're on Ohlone land right now, in solidarity with indigenous struggle everywhere.

A lot of the conversation around queering astrology has been about decolonizing the sky, as Chani so wisely said at one point during our preparation for this work. It is really important for me to recognize the ways that this patriarchal pantheon can change, grow and evolve to reflect more accurately who we are now as people. And so my talk tomorrow is on Asteroids, which is a really great way of bringing some Goddesses and queerness in.

Audience: What's your name?

Stella: I'm Stella, Stella the Good Witch. Thank you so much for asking what my name is. My full name is Stella Mystery and I feel like with a name like that I had to become an astrologer; my mom really knew who was coming. Thank you all for being here. I'm also facilitating the White Allies Caucus so I hope to see some of you there. Thank you.

Lilia: So part of the beauty of going last is that I get to have all these amazing people say things for me. My name is Lilia, and I just feel like all of you have said such good things and shone light on different facets of what astrology is. I just feel so lucky in this moment to have that resonating around me.

I work as a psychotherapist and have been using astrology kind of on the down low, and sometimes more obviously than others, and many of my clients have brought me their charts. I work a lot in the queer community and what I find is that so many people have been so deeply wounded by not being accurately mirrored and reflected by all of these different discourses, especially ones that are trying to show us who we are, and they are not showing us who we are. So there's so much healing possible as we delve into finding reflections that accurately reflect queer people.

I'm so excited by being really slow with the chart: How are you relating to that moon in Aries today? What is it like for you to really own that part of yourself and really become embodied in that part of yourself? And really work with all of the wars you have inside that part of yourself? That's kind of how I work.

My workshop is called Astro Drag and I really wanted to do something that was fun and embodied and to let people really play in all of the different ways that we are experiencing our charts in our bodies, and how that can grow and change. You can even step into someone else's chart for a little bit to experience something that is in someone else, to give everybody more space for who they are around gender and sexuality. I am so happy to be here.

Ian: In the spirit of turning the room around (*Walking to the back of the room, to greet a recent arrival*) we're all introducing ourselves and talking about the call that brought us here. Are you who I think you are? You're also speaking, so can I invite you into the conversation? (*Laughter*)

Yolo: Okay, you caught me off guard. Hi, my name is Yolo. I just got in late last night from New York so I am kind of in awe of the Bay Area realness that is happening right now. Wow, it's so amazing.

How do I begin? Just briefly, I started off with astrology, actually a partner of mine who, years ago, was really deep into astrology. At the time I was doing case management counseling at a community center with black gay men. I was really intellectual at that point. I was into Women's Studies and African American Studies so I was very critical and very intellectual. And what ended up happening is that I started doing risk assessment for all the young people who would come into the room.

When I did these risk assessments and got all this information, I looked for their birthdays, because I would try to see if I could assess or sense their sun sign based on this engagement with them. The engagement went beyond just the risk behaviors. It would also include things that happened, family, all this stuff. It got to the point where I was about seventy to eighty percent accurate, and I got a little scared. There was something happening here. So that was the beginning of my avenue into astrology.

In that context I was working with queer folks, with the LGBT folks, coming out of a feminist, womanist legacy. That is the work that I do. So the workshop I'll be doing today is called Queering Compatibility. Queering astrological compatibility is thinking about different ways we understand compatibility, not only the ways it is presented in pop culture, but also what we can do as practitioners.

It comes out of my experience being in an open relationship at one point with a Taurus, a Cancer, and a Capricorn, thinking this should never happen—how is this happening? And then thinking about me as a Libra and about the ways in which compatibility is understood in regards to elements and energies. But there is actually a lot of cultural bias in astrology when it comes to relationship structures, gender and power. So we'll be talking about that in the workshop that I'll be doing.

I am excited to meet you all. This is really great.

Ian: So we've got the next twenty minutes or so for questions or for other people who want to want to weigh in on what brought them to the "What's a Queer Astrology?" or "How do you queer astrology?" panel. Chani is going to moderate.

Audience: Patriarchy. (*Laughter*) Heteronormative. (*More laughter*)

Chani: My talk is on the inception of patriarchy, the beginning of it, just so I can say patriarchy again.

So does anyone have any questions for any of the presenters, or does anyone want to talk about patriarchy at all? (*Laughter*) Again we want this to be participatory.

Yolo: So years ago I worked at this organization called Men Stopping Violence and it's an organization that organizes men to work at ending violence against women. And one of the things we did was taught men's anger management classes, but they're commonly called batterers intervention courses.

So we're sitting in one group I was co-facilitating with a colleague of mine, and earlier that week we had been having a conversation about astrology and how that was being used in certain contexts. And I still remembered being so jarred by this: there was a gentleman in there—a lot of the gentlemen in there had been convicted of assault and battery and were in the program for 24 weeks—and so this one gentleman was used to the program. He comes in, we have this mandated kind of spiel we do. And he says, "People say, you know, I know that I am in here largely because I'm a Taurus and I get aggressive and sometimes I want to hit her." And I was like: "Whoa." (*Audience echoes "whoa"*)

And it was such a revelation suddenly, because first of all, we had never heard that come into the conversation. He really felt that so concretely. He felt, "I'm a Taurus. I get angry. When I charge, I have no control over it, and the zodiac and astrology actually confirm my violence and my aggression."

So of course, we went through the conversation. I gave him a look that said this is your work right here. And I had to get into a dialogue with him in a public space about astrology not being this fatalistic thing. "Oh, because you are this Taurus energy, there are violent ways that you are going to act, and you've become socialized that way, so that's ok?" This was very jarring to everybody else in the room. They were thinking, "Whoa what's happening right now? We're into astrology, what's going on?"

But this is a reality if we are talking about patriarchy and astrology. There is a way in which it is being used to justify really abusive and violent behaviors and that is really important to talk about in the context of being queer astrologers. (*Applause*)

Chani: Does anyone want to comment on what Yolo just said up on the panel?

Rhea: I have to say something. Even though I am thoroughly delighted every time somebody says the word patriarchy and that we are feeling like it is something that we are trying to slough off, shake off, leave behind and break its spell, I also have to say that patriarchy simply means the rule of the fathers, and matriarchy the rule of the mothers. I don't think inherently either one, when we break them down and define them, is bad: mother, father, parent, whatever.

So I guess I just want to bring into the Queer Astrology conversation the idea that there is something beyond and bigger than cultural patriarchy that we are trying to move out from under. Even identifying it negatively as other and putting ourselves in a fight against it can lead us instantly into a dichotomy that separates us from our queerness again. So I just wanted to say that. (*Applause*)

Audience: Hi, my name is Jenn. Following on that as well, what drew me here as a spectator was to see if all of the talks are going to be about essentialism, and what this topic brings to the questions of essentialism in astrology. It seems as though, instead of talking in terms of (*Whispers*) patriarchy, we can also think about: What is Essentialism?

Essentialism means there is a strict definition of the essence of something—that all things have a unique essence that can be defined. The topic of queering might actually subvert the idea that there is one way to be, and this is essential to being. Queering, on the other hand, suggests there are multiple ways of being that are not so tied to the physical manifestation of something versus our interpretation of it. The essence of Mars or the essence of asteroids as we interpret them, or the essence of gender—this is what it is to be male or this is what it is to be female, or whatever—and how then we interpret these things in our work or embody these essential definitions in ourselves, is all about to change. It seems as though there is perhaps an unquestioned essentialism in astrology that has been practiced up to this point and now we are about to break away from that—or not?

Chani: I wonder if any of what you are saying is about having reverence for the foundations of astrology? Or am I misreading your comment?

Audience: I don't think it is a matter of reverence for the foundation; I don't believe there is such thing as an essential astrology, actually. I think astrologers exist and there are many ways of doing astrology, or practicing astrology. So I think one reason why this conference has been called together, as a spectator of the field, is that there is a common assumption that there are only a certain few major branches of astrology, and some get published more than others, and more convened about than others. So we are thinking about ways to do astrology outside of that construct, but in terms of questioning these essential things having to do with strict definitions versus more inquiry and interpretation.

Audience: I just wanted to express my gratitude for this gathering, and I am grateful to be here, because, I am sure you can sympathize—I've got Saturn in Libra—and therefore there is this traditionalism and this desire to find, not necessarily the essentialist point, but where did it begin in antiquity? And what is the true astrology? Or what is the real thing?

In fact, I went all the way to Arizona for the AFA conference to take in this traditional way and the notion of not cracking this thing open and looking outside, where I must revere the ancestors and the way they practiced and interpreted astrology. I can't help myself, but in the end I can't just look at externals, external forms—that's where Saturn in Libra comes in—I look at the formal beauty of things that are in the past and forms that are present. But yes, I want to be allowed to break that open and to break it open with you people and come out of all that. As Ian said, it's important to come out, but there is a constant coming out, because we're always coming out as all kinds of things, like having Saturn in Libra. (*Laughter*)

Lilia: I just want to respond to what you said, Erin, around "What it is." And I think one of things that I am really excited about is changing the perspective from "What it is" to "How we're relating to it."

Christopher: Yolo, I was fascinated actually by the comment you were making about that fellow. Was he talking about being fated to be that way? Or was he typing himself? Because astrology is, for good or bad, kind of responsible as the first form of personality profiling, when you take into account the different planets, the different signs, the different temperaments.

And I was very intrigued about that and whether that was something that was coming into the dialogue at all. One of the reasons is that there a woodcut from the fifteenth century that demonstrates the choleric temperament, and it is literally a husband beating his wife. That is the image in the woodcut if anyone is familiar with that.

So I wonder also as we explore this kind of dialogue how much are we talking about the time-old issues in astrology of fate versus free will, or rather that fate may be coordinating and working with free will? But also the elements of personality typing or profiling—saying I am like this because I am queer, or I am like this because I am straight, or I am like this because I am upper-middle class, or I am like this because I have been disenfranchised or something along those lines. It came up as an idea.

Yolo: Yes, in this particular instance, what was interesting was the way he couched it. It was not necessarily that his temperament was aggressive, but this was a consequence of his temperament. It was almost like he was suggesting that "because I am a Taurus this action of assaulting her, of being aggressive to her, is something that is an immutable aspect of who I am and is going to remain so." Which is what was troubling to me. The way in which I tried to engage him is like what you were saying, that "OK, so you understand this is your temperament; however, the choices that you make based on this temperament are not fated or dictated by astrology. Astrology does not say that you are a Taurus, therefore it is acceptable for you to assault your partner." I think that is what he was getting at that was really troubling to me. And I've seen that happen in a number of other situations with various different aspects of personality. So I think it is important to talk about action versus embodiment. How we may feel our temperament may be versus the choices that we make in terms of how we respond to that. I think that was a big concern for me.

Barry: I sort of want to piggyback on what Jenn was saying about essentialism, because I think it cuts to the core of what I find to be one of the most interesting questions and intellectual problems that we face as queer astrologers, which is that astrology is a metaphysical art or craft. We believe that we possess some access to some sort of truth that nobody knows where it comes from. There are a lot of smarty pants astrologers in this room (*Laughter*), but I promise you that there is not a single one of us who can explain to anybody how astrology works, because there is a huge beautiful metaphysical mystery at the heart of what it is that we do here, that we could describe as essential, or archetypal, or something similar. But it is transcendent in some way. That is why we all ended up here: At some point we all had a transcendent moment with astrology that blew our minds wide open and we wanted to hear more.

On the other hand, queering is a very academic method that deconstructs the structures of knowledge by identifying the particular bias being pushed by a particular person in a particular position of power. Our job as "queerers" is to explain what that bias is in astrology and what is going on there. So there is a conflict in some way, sort of ontologically, between dealing with a metaphysical craft and dealing with an intellectual process by which we are trying to deconstruct something. Typically, when there is a metaphysical or religious belief that shows up in the queer theory class, it is the academic's job to pick apart that structure and explain why that is a dogma being pushed so that the people in power can continue being in power.

But if we believe in astrology then we believe that there is something that happens above, or transcends, that power structure that is somehow between us and the sentient universe. And so, when we are trying to deconstruct something about astrology, by definition, we are trying to deconstruct the essentialist model. That is a tricky proposition. So we are all being charged as pioneers with a very tricky proposition that I think we should draw attention to as opposed to try and squirrel our way out of. (*Applause*)

Audience: I'm Nora Jean Stone and I'm the Director of Publicity and Outreach for the San Francisco Astrological Society. And I'm a feral astrologer. (*Applause*) An Archy and Mehitable, for those who are old enough to know.

I'd like to make a differentiation between metaphysical and religious. When people say: Do you believe in astrology I say: No! (*Laughter*) I practice astrology. I take a hammer and I hit a nail. I don't have to believe in the nail, I don't have to believe in the hammer. I don't have to worship the saw. I use it. It's a tool. OK?

The reason why it is metaphysical is because we don't know how it works. I don't know how an airplane works, but I'll fly to Tucson. (*Laughter*) People split hairs about, "Is it technical?" Just stop it! I'm not going to say it is just because I have Mercury conjunct Saturn in Virgo in the 8th. I just ask, "Is it practical? Can you use it? Does it work?"

Don't believe it out of hand, because that's crap. That is when you keep re-eating the vomit. It keeps regurgitating over and over and over—people copying shit from these old dead trees. (*Roaring laughter*)

Now I'm not queer. I have a gay son, and so I am sympathetic. I am an ally. But what I am is a radical woman. And I don't like patriarchy telling me what to do. I don't like patriarchy telling me what to believe, and saying: "squares are bad." No, squares are work. "Trines are good." No, trines make you lazy. OK?

We have to rethink everything that we've been told by our experience when we do readings for other people. Instead of regurgitating that which has been told to you, think about what you've seen with other people. Ask yourself, "Does this hold up?" If it doesn't it is time to throw it away because it is out of fashion.

So whether it does not hold up because of our sexuality, or because of feminist liberation, or because we are people of color, or short, or old, then if it doesn't work throw it away. If it works, keep it. But by all means, question everything you read and put it up against what you know, what you see, with your readings and the people you deal with.

Suspect everyone of bullshit.

Audience: On a side note, I was going to ask people to maybe be mindful of the type of language that they are using in order to make sure everyone accesses the knowledge here. Because I imagine there is a lot of different levels and types of education that are present in this room. So a lot of the academic language that is being used might not be familiar to people. So if you could work on defining more of the big words you are using, that might be helpful to some people. (*Applause*)

Audience: Hello, my name is Steve, and I'm trying to see the queer movement as the vanguard of an equality movement which will transcend all the differences. To me, the equality movement is an Aquarian age ideal. Now, along with that, we have other Aquarian age things happening right now. With Uranus being so prominent with Pluto, it seems to be a time of activism; for example, the Supreme Court's recent decision regarding marriage equality, et cetera.

And I actually have a question for Rod. In terms of the age, that is, the Piscean age going into the Aquarian age, the Piscean has been both patriarchal and spiritual at the same time. For example, the Catholic Church is the epitome of the last two thousand years of Piscean culture. And now we're going to the Aquarian age. What is the transition? When does it start or when did it start? And are these age transitions instantaneous, or do they take a while to happen?

Rod: Oh yeah! That's a really interesting question. I guess I feel as if this happened in the 1780s when Uranus was discovered. That the world went through an incredible transformation during that century, at the end of that century that laid the foundation for us having a queer liberation movement at all.

There have been many dates for the Aquarian age, so it's hard to say exactly when the transition occurs. But, of course, Uranus is thought to rule Aquarius and they are certainly consonant with each other archetypally, so its discovery and after is important. As I have been doing my research, I think more and more that both astrology and queers are queer-Uranians. And Uranian used to be the name for queers. So I feel like our job in this world, in this universe, is, I don't want to talk essentialist point of view, but in some way we're here to shake things up. We're here to do gender bending. We're here to do modeling for people about how to do live differently. I think we need to be catalysts. I think we are. Everywhere we go, every action we do, every room we walk into. We are perceived as different, as other, and that's our job in the universe in a lot of ways. I think that's a Uranian function, a Uranus function.

As I'll also show in my talk, in the 1780s things changed for us. And it's been a steady progression, so these things do take time. I kind of expect this to take about five hundred years, to be honest. But this has never happened before in the history of humanity, what we are experiencing right now. Never. I'll say more about that later.

Audience: I'd like to mention one word I haven't heard yet is Capitalism. Something that is bringing me here that has put me on a search for radical astrologers is my commitment to working towards a world with more equal resource distribution. I think the patriarchy is connected to capitalism, but I think that the unequal distribution of resources is the most serious thing, in my opinion. I am really interested in using astrology as a tool for social movements, for planning and implementing actions. I think it can be really useful. I want astrology to be legitimate in the academy and in activist movements and so that's important to me, that's why I'm here.

Stella: Thank you for naming that; I really appreciate it. I work with a lot of activists and healers, and I feel like it is one thing that is often times missing in astrology is a political analysis of any kind, and a willingness to really go there with people. And one of the things that made me really excited about being involved with this conference is that it is a way that we can bring our political and spiritual selves together. Yeah. And I think this relates to the conversation that is happening about essentialism as well.

Another thing that is really important for me with client work is working with a lot of co-ops. It is amazing what can happen in terms of understanding how people are communicating differently, in order to create a better tomorrow today.

And I think part of it is by talking about agency. There's a way that essentialism in astrology–the example that Yolo gave, and I've had experiences myself with Tauruses who were engaged in domestic violence–is coming from a place in astrology that is important to identify. There is a way that the oppressive expression of any spiritual practice, of any kind of work, happens when we remove our agency from the conversation, and our right to own and have authority for our own lives. And so I start every session I have with a client giving them back that authority and saying: "You are the ultimate authority on your life. Take what resonates, leave what doesn't." (*Applause*)

Chani: Anyone have a burning question? Statement?

Rhea: When I was talking to astrologers up at the Northwest Astrological Conference outside of Seattle about the Queer Astrology Conference, and telling them that it was happening, people were really excited to hear about it.

But we also were kind of joking around a little bit about what you were just saying about the Uranian energy of both the queer community and astrology. And we were joking, wondering if two Uranuses make a Saturn? Like, "OK, is this going to be two weirds coming together and getting really rigid?" And we were laughing about it but I think it was a good point, too, for us to think about. How do we keep queering this conference?

For me it means to keep leaning into the questions and away from certainty. (*Yes!*) To me that is an essential component of what Queer Astrology is. I keep leaning into the questions. If I think I know something then I am going in the wrong direction.

Ian: So here we are, and that's wonderful. I want to take a moment for acknowledgments...I'd like those of us who were at the first meeting to raise a hand. (*Applause*) We've been getting this together over the last four months. And now people who joined in at the later meetings, and now everyone who was here at the volunteer meeting yesterday. (*Loud clapping*)

Thank you all, and enjoy the day.

The Saturn Return of AIDS

Christopher Renstrom

Image 1: Silence = Death

THANK you for coming and attending today's lecture, which is "The Saturn Return of AIDS." I was in the middle of my Saturn Return when I lost my partner Brian Greenbaum to AIDS. Brian and I met at a friend's birthday party in New York in 1985. I was twenty-four and Brian was twenty-three. Brian was an expatriate living in Germany at the time and making films. He was in New York acting as a location scout. A graduate of Brown University, Brian majored in economics and semiotics. Brian was best described as an enfant terrible. Brian was worldly, intellectual, and uproariously funny. He still had a bit too much of the seven-year-old boy genius running around inside him for his own good. Brian also had the curious knack for being in the right place at the right time but never recognizing it. He moved back to New York months after we met so that we could be together. Once settled back in New York, Brian produced a number of independent films and launched the careers of his Brown classmates Christine Vachon, founder of Killer Films, and the filmmaker Todd Haynes.

Brian was diagnosed with AIDS in 1987, and what followed from that point on was basically five years of hell. We had health insurance maybe because of TEIGIT,[1] he was in film, the independent film industry. We basically had no rights, and medical therapy for him was catch-as-catch-can. I don't know if there are many people in this room who remember the '80s, or the '90s, but if you were diagnosed positive they handed you AZT and/or a Band-Aid, it might have been the same thing. And as I was saying earlier, this was the time that I also began practicing astrology.

We began the lying in 1986 and '87. And we began the covering up with makeup for him–he would get KS[2] on his face–at that time as well. And you lied to your friends, and you lied to your family, and you lied to the closest people to you, because you couldn't trust if anyone was going to gossip or give you away–and that might mean loss of employment, loss of health insurance, loss of your apartment…so you did what you could. Suddenly you were living in an alien country, all as a result of this illness.

So, to go through a Saturn Return–you know, when you would open up the textbooks and they would say, "this is the time when you were leaving behind your childhood and you're entering into adulthood," well, that had very strong impact during the period of time. What had come before was completely nonexistent, and what would come next you really didn't know. Brian died on February 29, 1992–it was a leap year–at 12:05 or 12:15 in the morning. (It's that astrologer's habit to always go and look at the clock whenever something is going on.)

---

1. The Entertainment Industry Group Insurance Trust
2. Kaposi's sarcoma

So, when I was invited to come speak at this conference, what struck me for the first time was that AIDS was going through its Saturn Return. And so there was this kind of Saturn Return/Saturn Return thing going on. So what I wanted to do was to draw up a horoscope for AIDS. Anything that is born into this world has a horoscope, including a pandemic, and so the next problem then became: how do you decide the birth day? Of course there was evidence that it was first being reported in 1981; there were traces of it earlier in the twentieth century, etc. But what I decided to go with was the naming of the virus itself, when the virus was named AIDS. The AIDS virus was named for the first time at a meeting at FDA headquarters in Washington D.C. This is documented in the book *And the Band Played On* by Randy Shilts. I decided, well let's take a look at that, you know—let's see what that will tell us about the virus and what kind of questions one might have about this virus. And so what you see on page 30 (Image 2) is the horoscope for the AIDS virus.

My initial impulse was actually to draw it for twelve noon, for the middle of the day. But thanks to Missy Hunt at USFDA, Virginia Rosenberg, who is a research associate of mine, and Richard Klein and Steven Warren at the CDC, we were able to come up with an approximation, because of course I was asking, and in their mind this meeting where it was named was really kind of inconsequential; like, "why do you want to know the time of day anyway? And what is all of this about?" But with some finagling and conversing, they asked people who asked other people. I do have to tell you the time is passed down from someone who essentially said, "I'm pretty sure that we came up with the name after lunch break."...that's pretty much when there was a consensus that the AIDS name would be much better than, for instance, GRID, which stood for Gay-Related Immune Deficiency at the time, and so AIDS would be more generic-sounding. If you were alive during that time you probably realized it was the death knell for the popular diet candy, which was called AIDS because it was supposed to aid you in losing weight. That was the end of that product. So, I hedged my bets and decided on a 2 p.m. time to draw the horoscope. So the AIDS virus is July 27, 1982, Bethesda, Maryland, and I drew it for 2 p.m.

This is a meeting that was not called by a gay group. It was called by Bruce Evatt, who was the director of hematology for the Centers for

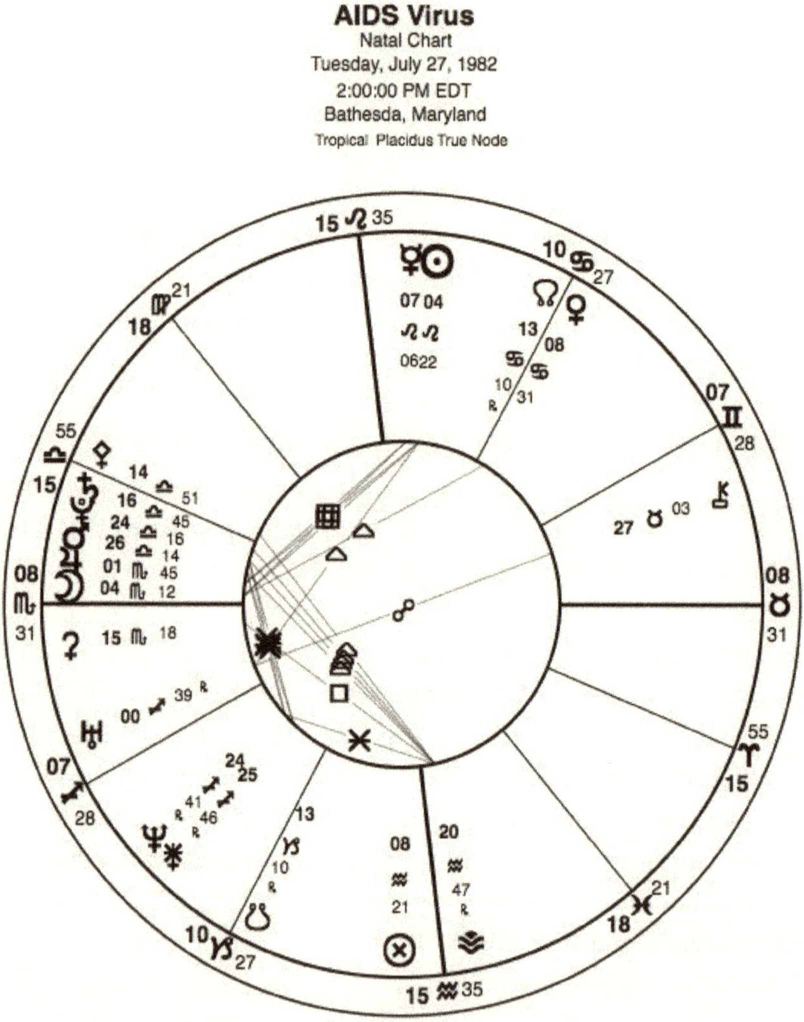

AIDS Virus
Natal Chart
Tuesday, July 27, 1982
2:00:00 PM EDT
Bathesda, Maryland
Tropical Placidus True Node

Image 2: AIDS Virus Chart

Disease Control. He was concerned about the blood banks, the national blood banks. And so that's why this meeting was called. So actually we begin with hemophilia, which is why he called the meeting. Hemophilia is a genetic disorder that impairs the body's ability to clot blood. It is usually passed down to males. It featured prominently in European royalty and was thus known as "the royal disease." Queen Victoria—if you've read Linea van Horn's article "Blinded by the Light"—known as the grandmother of Europe, passed it on to every one of her children, who married into the royal families of Spain, Germany, and Russia. Queen Victoria had nine children, and this is why hemophilia became connected to the royal disease. Hemophilia was basically internal bleeding, or if you cut yourself you could not stop bleeding because the blood would not clot, but actually I believe the main killer was internal bleeding that went on, on the inside. Improvements in transfusion technology during World War II allowed so that hemophiliac patients could receive infusions of fresh whole blood or fresh frozen plasma containing the missing clotting factor, so this actually transformed the lives of hemophiliacs—until that point you were lucky if you lived to the age of thirty. I believe the average age of death was somewhere around eleven to fourteen. OK, so that post-WWII, as technology improved, life expectancy improved, so that by 1980 if you were a hemophiliac, a sufferer of hemophilia, your life expectancy could actually be relatively normal, about sixty.

So, the plasma demand rose significantly during this period of time. Plasma—that is, people giving blood—came from the extremely poor, alcoholics, basically what was generally considered outsiders or the dregs of society.

The screening at this period of time—we're really talking about the '80s right now—was not particularly tight, or scrutinized, or studied. In fact, what would happen is that hemophiliacs would often get Hepatitis from these blood transfusions, and that was kind of deemed "all right." A doctor would sit down and say, as a result of this transfusion of blood you may get Hepatitis, and Hepatitis was manageable, was treatable, or regarded that way, so it became the happy trade-off. "If that's what I have to do to get the blood that will allow me to live, well then that's all right, that's a trade-off that I'm willing to make."

So here I want to read about what brings this meeting together. Actually, what brings this meeting together is that prior to July of 1982, Pneumocystis pneumonia, known by the initials PCP, showed up in the blood of a hemophiliac, and so there was concern because PCP was one of the opportunistic infections that was connected to GRID, which is what AIDS was called at the time. There was concern. How did something that affected one part of the population, why was it now showing up in another part of the population? And so Evatt, who was director of Hematology, began going over files and cases and sort of he came up with what was kind of called at the time, the 4H Club, in which this was starting to show up: hemophiliacs, homosexuals, Haitians, and heroin users. There was actually a fifth—in the black humor of the doctors of the time—whores, but it didn't begin with an H; it technically began with a W.

So, this meeting is called, on July 27, 1982, and here I read from *The Tragic History of AIDS in the Hemophilia Population* by B. L. Evatt:

> On the 27th of July the CDC representatives met with a group of leaders from the blood industry: hemophilia groups, gay community organizations, and representatives from the NIH (National Institute of Health) and FDA (Food and Drug Administration), to present the evidence of a possible transmission by a blood-borne agent. If the attendees accepted this possibility, we reasoned that high-risk groups should be prohibited from donating blood until the issue could be clarified by future studies. It was a long day. Detailed histories of hemophiliac cases were systematically presented, followed by data from the other risk groups—only the high risk for blood-borne infections could explain a risk common to all four groups. But, rather than expressing alarm at a possible blood-borne infection, and

suggesting ways to reduce a blood-borne risk, the audience expressed an almost universal reluctance to act. The scientific community had yet to see published evidence that the syndrome was indeed an infectious disease, let alone blood-borne and sexually transmitted, homosexuals were major blood donors in the large cities on the east and west coasts. It was thought that singling out homosexuals for exclusion would unnecessarily stigmatize them without evidence that they were indeed transmitting the disease. The blood industry, threatened by losing a large donor pool, strongly supported the position of the gay groups on this issue. Three hemophilia patients with the syndrome did not mean that they should spend millions of dollars changing recruitment and screening practices. The hemophiliac groups expressed concerns that the data showing immune suppression in hemophiliac patients could have reflected the effects of prolonged use of blood products and did not necessarily mean that they had the new syndrome. They also feared the stigma of having a disease associated with homosexual patients and were concerned that reducing the use of clotting factor concentrates would bring back old issues of deformities and early death. The FDA, which had regulatory authority over the blood industry—and when we're talking about the blood industry here, we're talking about the Red Cross, one of the prominent companies that was here at this meeting—had not yet accepted the collection of disorders related to immune deficiency as a single disease and was also skeptical that hemophiliac patients represented another risk group. Thus, no consensus was reached concerning blood donors. However, the meeting did accomplish one thing: and that was to name the virus AIDS. (Evatt, 2006)

Queer Astrology Anthology

Image 3: Sol and His Children

So in the horoscope of AIDS, and as you can see right off the bat, AIDS is a Leo. (*Long pause, audience laughter*) I don't know about you, but that's not exactly the sign I would have chosen for it. As you see in the chart, Leo is in the 9th House–the Sun is in the 9th House, in the zodiac sign of Leo. So I started to do some digging around and discovered that, for instance, the Sun is in its Joy in the 9th House, meaning that is a very powerful placement for it. The 9th House is connected to prophecy. It is connected to long journeys, long travel, traveling out into the world. It's also, as Deborah Houlding refers to in her book *Temples in the Sky*, a moral house. It is a house that is very much connected to moral values and moral concerns.

What you'll see in Image 3 is a wood block from the 15th century, which is called "Sol and His Children." There were different wood blocks that were illustrated at this time; you have "The Sun and His Children," "The Moon and Her Children," "Venus and Her Children," and "Mars and His Children," and these were basically illustrations of the different castes of society, or different ways of life or lifestyles that could be expected if you were born under that ruling planet. The poem which accompanies the woodcut reads:

Image 4: *Lovers of the Sun* by Henry Scott Tuke

Men call me Sol,
I am the sun,
The middle planet,
on I run.
Beneficent
and warm and warm and dry,
By nature my rays
fill the sky.
The Lion's my house,
therein I dwell,
And brightly shining
I do well.
There I stand,
fair and bold,
Against old Saturn's
bitter cold.
In the Ram I rule and reign,
But in the Maid I fail, I wane.
And through the stars my way to wend,
Three hundred and sixty-five days I spend.

Noble and fortunate I am,
As are all my children.
Good beards, large foreheads, bodies fair,
Ruddy lips, of brains their share.
Happy, kindly, well-born, strong,
Fond of harps, viols, and song.
All morning long to God they pray,
And after noon they laugh and play.
They wrestle and they fence with swords,
They throw great stones, and serve great lords.
Manly exercises are their sports,
They have good luck in princely courts.

Basically, what this was talking about were the favored children of the zodiac. What you'll notice in that wood cut is that it's almost all male. There really isn't a woman to be seen anywhere. And they're out on public display. They're picking up stones and heaving them, because it's like discus throwing. Or there's sword play. Or they're doing athletics. And these are things that we associate with Leo, or the 5th House pleasures; these are the things that we connect with that sign.

So Apollo is a god that's associated with the arts and creative expression. He's the leader of the Muses, so he's the god of arts and sciences. The laurel wreath is beloved to him as a symbol of his honor and the lyre

Image 5: Belvedere Apollo

represents the music that he plays. This was very important because there were two musical instruments in ancient Greece. There was the flute or pan-pipes, and the lyre. If you played the flute, you were in the lower part of society, because when you were playing the flute you could not speak. If you played the lyre, you spoke. So this idea of a being civilized through 'lyrics', that is, words that are spoken while playing the lyre, or having status through speaking poetry, is connected to Apollo and his lyre.

Apollo is the favorite child of Zeus, the only one who knew Zeus's mind and spoke it. And Apollo was the god of healing, father to Asclepius the god of medicine. Apollo is connected to golden youth, the Ephebes. Ephebes were young men between the ages of fifteen and nineteen, and they wore their hair long. They wore their hair piled up on top, and then long down the back. You can see how they wore it in Image 5 of the Belvedere Apollo sculpture. Apollo represented—and you can see it in this sculpture—the epitome of the classic Greek youth.

He's the most Greek of all the Greek gods, so it's this beautiful male body, athletic, gorgeous, and golden. What you do not see here because it has been cracked off or for whatever reason no longer there, is that Apollo is actually holding the weapon which is most connected to him, which is the bow and arrow. You can see it here in his right hand—that is the bow—and so this hand is actually pulling back the string. And he's rather sashaying a little bit. (*Laughter*) So he's connected to arrows.

In *Marginal Waters #9* by Chicago photographer Doug Ischar, which is Image 6 and came out in 1985, we see symbols of the youth and hope of the time. The late 1970s and early 1980s were a time of incredible liberation and celebration. This was when the social and sexual revolution for the gay community was just gaining momentum. After years of living in the closet and facing public arrest and humiliation, the gay community was seizing the opportunity to live and love as they pleased. It may have appeared hedonistic to some, but for us it was like a Utopian dream come true.

Image 6: *Marginal Waters #9*, 1985 by Doug Ischar.
Photo appears courtesy of Doug Ischar.

Apollo was seen as the protector of young men, with the long hair. And when young men actually made the transition from youth to manhood, they would cut off their hair and they would present it to Apollo as tribute. And so Apollo collected the young hair of men.

Apollo was also the destroyer of young men. He was known as the killer of young men, with the bow and arrow. And that comes from the myth involving Niobe, who very foolishly boasts that she has more children than Leto. Niobe had nine or twelve children, and Leto only had two–Diana and Apollo–who were both archers. And so in vengeance, because she'd shown hubris, Diana and Apollo slay Niobes' children: Apollo slayed the young boys; Diana, the young women. So these are two gods or archetypes that are set up as protective figures but also slaying figures of a particular part of society: young adolescents. Apollo was both a slayer and a protective deity. Apollo was the god who protected your city.

Image 7: Apollo with Bow and Arrow

What I did discover, in the first chapter of *The Iliad*–if anyone remembers that from high school–is Apollo is also the god of plagues. He sends plagues through his burning arrows. And in fact, *The Iliad* begins with Homer saying Agamemnon has captured some Trojan priestess. Troy was sacred to Apollo, and Athena I believe was fighting on the side of the Greeks. So Agamemnon takes a priestess' daughter and makes her a sex slave, and that's what she is to him, and so the Trojan priest comes, asking for his daughter to be released to him. He comes with Apollo's staff and the golden ribbons that are connected, and Agamemnon has the attitude, "Old man get out of my face. Heh heh heh, I'm going to have my way with your daughter and I'm going to do it right here in front of you if you stick around–heh heh heh." And so the old man walks away, erratically down the beach weaving this way and that in his futility, which mimics the action of the surf, and he cries out to Apollo.

And Apollo came, Homer says, as night comes, and let go an arrow. Terrible was the clash that rose from the bow of silver. First he went after the mules and the circling hounds. And then let go a tearing arrow against the men themselves (that's Agamemnon's soldiers) and struck them. The corpse fires burned everywhere, and they did not stop burning. Apollo is connected to the Semitic god Raseph, who was also a plague god who shot fire-brands, fiery arrows that sent plagues, and Raseph's sacred animal was the lion, which accompanied him. And Raseph was connected or associated in people's minds to Apollo. So, Apollo is a protector, a healer, a bringer of plagues, and a purifier. Apollo basically revokes immunity. He revokes protection, and makes vulnerable the body, makes vulnerable the men and women who were infected with this virus, so that what resides in the body as a harmless organism—something which no one thought twice about—all of a sudden takes on a very slow and lethal ascendancy.

Let me read to you from my copy of the Gay Men's Health Crisis Pamphlet: Medical Answers About AIDS to give you some idea of what the gay community was dealing with:

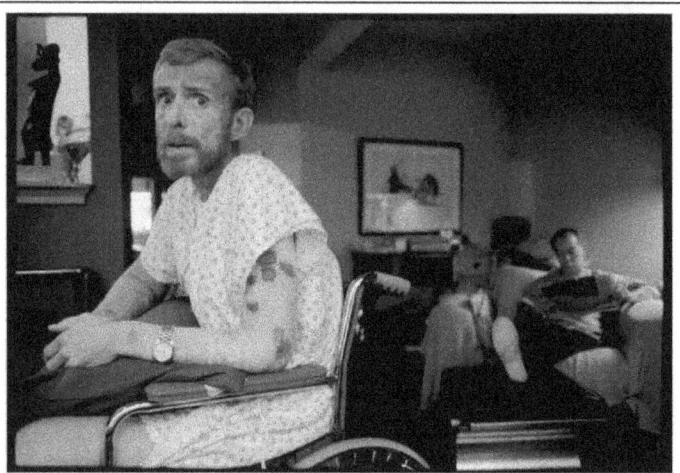

Image 8: *Ken Meeks with KS.* By Kevin Meeks
© Alon Reininger/(Contact Press Images)

PCP is the most common life-threatening infection in a person with AIDS. About half the people with AIDS first manifest the syndrome by getting this disease. And almost all will develop it during the course of their illness. Along with KS (which is what you see all over the gentleman in Image 8), and many other conditions, it is one of the criteria used by the Centers for Disease Control to define the presence of AIDS itself. PCP is a parasitic protozoan infection of the lungs, with symptoms similar to any other pneumonia: high fever, shortness of breath, and in this case a dry cough. It seldom infects people who do not have AIDS. Although PCP is a very common organism that is present in most people, it just does not cause disease in those with normal health.

CMV, the virus, is a common infection in a person with AIDS. It's actually a virus commonly found in homosexual men, but it's usually harmless. Its exact role in the development of AIDS is not well understood. In persons with AIDS, CMV can appear in the eyes, lungs, brain, or colon. Or it may attack other bodily organs, including the trachea or the liver. If left untreated in the eyes it can cause loss of vision. In the colon or intestines it can cause chronic diarrhea, wasting, and very painful cramps. Until recently there was no treatment for CMV. Early in the AIDS epidemic persons with CMV usually died slow, painful and wasting deaths. Often they went blind.

Toxo is another parasitic infection that attacks people with AIDS. It is found all over the world and lives in many people in a latent state causing no symptoms. In AIDS patients it usually invades the nervous system, especially the brain, resulting in seizures, high fevers, and a decreasing level of consciousness. Toxo used to be one of the more life-threatening and frightening infections that occurred in persons with AIDS since continued infection can lead to immobility and the inability to speak. However, thanks to new treatments it is less threatening but still very dangerous.

And finally KS, as the disease is called, is a cancer of the small blood vessels of the body and usually first appears as red blotches on the skin, which then turn into purplish-red lesions, hard to the touch, raised above the level of the surrounding skin. They often show up first on the arms or legs but can spread to the chest, back, face and neck. They also appear in the mouth and throat, where they become more dangerous. And eventually they can appear in internal organs such as the intestines, colon, or the lungs. (Mass, 1989)

Apollo is a bisexual god. He has dalliances with women, but he's rather famous for liking boys, and usually these are Ephebes, who are young boys between the ages of fifteen and eighteen. There is a famous story, the story of Hyacinthus, who gives birth to the flower (hyacinth), of whom Ovid says, "There was another boy who might have had a place in heaven, at Apollo's order, had fate seen fit to give him time, and still he is in his own fashion an immortal. It was noon one day. Apollo and Hyacinthus stripped, rubbed themselves with oil, and tried their skill at discus throwing. Apollo sent the missile far through the air, so far that it pierced the clouds. It took a long time coming down. And when it fell, it proved both his strength and skill. And Hyacinthus, all eager for his turn, heedless of danger, went running to pick it up, before it settled fully to earth. It bounced once and struck him full in the face, and he grew deadly pale, and as Apollo took up the huddled body, trying to warm the dreadful chill that held it, he cried, 'I see your wound. My crime. You are my sorrow, my reproach, my hand has been your murderer! But how am I to blame? Where is my guilt, except in playing with you, in loving you?'"

Image 9: The Death of Hyacinthus

So these are the somehow complementary, somehow contradictory ideas that I want to introduce around the Sun and around Apollo. What you will also see—and again thanks to Linea van Horn for her wonderful article, "Blinded by the Light," which I strongly, strongly recommend, she pointed out to me in a discussion that we had that Mercury is combust in the AIDS virus chart. When a planet is combust (within 8 degrees of the Sun) it can't be seen, because it is literally in the beams of the Sun. You cannot see it. The Sun blocks it out. And so, essentially, a planet that is combust is not able to do its job. What is Mercury but the planet of communication. And the idea of "Silence = Death," or not communicating, becomes an ongoing theme in the chart as you begin to sort of pick apart its strands. Mercury rules the 8th House, which is the house of death, and also the 11th House, which is the house of fraternity, your friends, the company that you keep. So here you get introduced to the idea of death coming through the company that you keep. And also the idea that it's not going to be communicated—if you remember that passage that I read aloud to you from Dr. Evatt's report—the decision on this day is, "We're not going to talk about it." So here the AIDS chart (Image 2) reflects, "We are not going to talk about this, all right?"

Now we get into what I was kind of expecting to see maybe as a Sun sign or something: Scorpio. And here you see it as Scorpio Rising. And so you've got the sign of sex and death, as well as other people's money, rising. We see the Moon, and we see Jupiter, rising in the zodiac sign of Scorpio. First of all, Scorpio...I work with Scorpio as being ruled by two planets, maybe it's my crazy thing, but I actually work with both of them as the ruler of Scorpio. I work with both Mars and Pluto, Eros and Thanatos, sex and death as connected to the ruler of the zodiac sign.

I also see Scorpio as being connected—because of Pluto—to wealth, but also it is connected to the 8th House which is other people's resources, other people's money. I don't think it's a big stretch to draw on the idea of banks, it's not money that belongs to you,

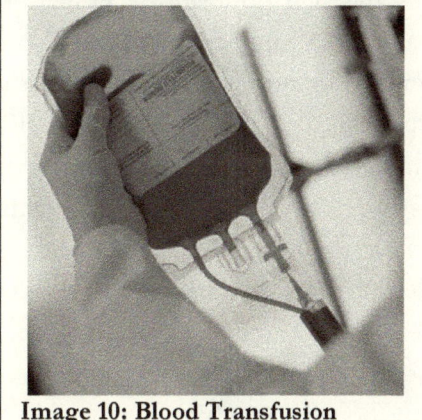

Image 10: Blood Transfusion

but money or resources that belongs to another. Jupiter rising in Scorpio. According to J. Lee Lehman, Judith Hill and Henry Cornell's book *Medical Astrology*, Jupiter is the planet of semen, and it is also the planet of blood. But there is a very important distinction: Jupiter is arterial blood, meaning blood that is inside. It is not blood that is spilled. That is Mars. Mars is spilled blood. But Jupiter is blood that is inside.

The idea of things being frozen, or put to one side, or in safe keeping, to my imagination, connects to Pluto, cryogenics, the idea of things being buried, or interred, or held for a long period of time, whether it is a grave or a blood bank, or human organisms. This begins to bring up this theme. So, for me, this was bringing up the idea of blood, blood transfusion, blood banks, specifically in keeping with what was going on with this CDC meeting that the AIDS horoscope was cast for. This is directly what is being reflected by Jupiter. Jupiter is also connected to the polis, the city-state; he's king of the gods, so Jupiter would also be government and the idea of governance. It leaves the question as to whether this wealth, this hidden resource (i.e. the blood banks) was being well-governed or not.

The Moon is also the body politic. When we look at a lunar eclipse, that's going to deal with the welfare of the state, but not the heads of state (which would be a solar eclipse, the Sun), but the body state, the people that make up the common folk. So here we see the Moon in fall. It's the sign opposite its exaltation in Taurus, rising in Scorpio, right behind the Jupiter. The Moon also rules the breasts and the womb. Very quickly–or not very quickly–the rulers of Scorpio, Mars and Pluto, go into the 12th House, and the 12th House is the house of hidden enemies, and the house of self-undoing. It rules over hospitals, prisons, asylums, rehab, and the disenfranchised. To me this talks about the area of concern–the state of the blood banks regarding hemophiliacs. It also describes the donors to those blood banks, people whom Dr. Evatt regards as being the dregs of society in his report, i.e. "the extremely poor, prisoners, alcoholics, etc."

So what you have here is "Sex = Death." You are infected with the hidden enemy. It's being carried around inside your body. Your lover becomes your killer, or you become his. You don't know this. And making love brings about your self-undoing.

So again, referring to the AIDS chart, we have Scorpio rising symbolizing the hidden face of the AIDS virus and the Leo Sun which is very exposed and seen. Indeed there was nothing subtle or slow acting about the opportunistic infections. They transformed your appearance dramatically. They branded their victims—particularly Kaposi's sarcoma—because you wore it. It was on your face. It was on your arms. There was no way that you were not going to be outed by this disease.

The other thing that sort of strikes me as intriguing is that Scorpio and Libra used to be one constellation, one star, until it was divided by the Romans to fit their twelve month calendar. And so basically, in Arabic, the northern claw of the scorpion was called Zubeneschamali and the southern claw was called Zubenelgenubi, and these claws of the scorpion became the scales of Libra. So there is this idea of connecting the themes of Libra and Scorpio together, so that you get the idea of the prick, the sting. The prick and the sting is following the scorpion, which actually becomes a sort of larger idea here, with the lineup of planets of Libra and the scorpion rising, but you also get the prick of the arrow that is being shot into, and so the idea of prick, prick of the arrow, prick of the penis, the prick of the needle, this idea of the pricking is showing up here, to my mind, in the chart itself.

Audience: I notice there is also a stellium in the Via Combusta, and I didn't know about the constellations being separate, and I was wondering if that was related to the Via Combusta?

Christopher: Yes. The area between 15^0 Libra and 15^0 Scorpio is termed the *Via Combusta*, the "Fiery Road" or "Combust Way." It is considered to be a debilitating area, particularly detrimental to the Moon. The definition of Via Combusta from Deborah Houlding's website Skyscript.co.uk reads:

The Astrologer Al Biruni wrote of it: "The Combust Way is the last part of Libra and the first of Scorpio. These two signs are not congenial to the Sun and the Moon on account of the obscurity and ill-luck connected with them and because each of them is the fall of one of the luminaries. They also contain the two malefics, the one by exaltation (Libra, Saturn) the other by house (Scorpio, Mars)."

I would also like to point out that Saturn is exalted in Libra in the AIDS chart and that Mars is in detriment.

HIV can be transmitted through three ways: Non-sexually by mixing contaminated blood or blood products with one's own blood, usually by injection; by sexual intercourse through the exchange of blood, semen, or vaginal secretions containing the virus; or by the

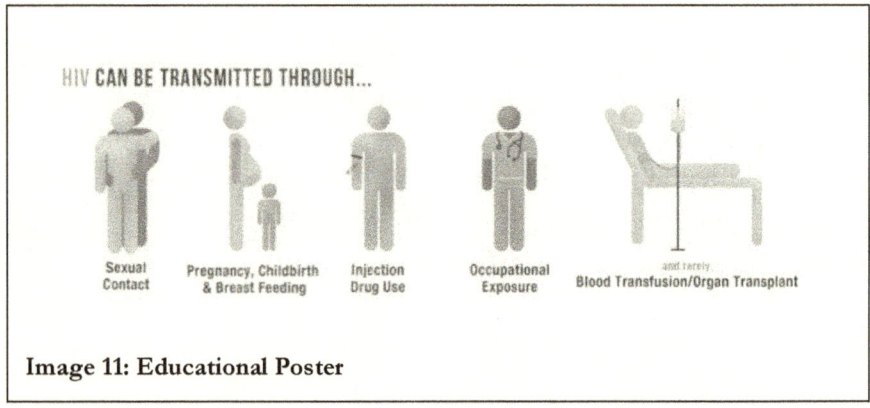

Image 11: Educational Poster

exchanges that occur between an infected mother and baby during pregnancy, birth, or breast feeding. There I want to address the Moon rising in Scorpio. What you'll see there, it can be transmitted sexually, or through injection, or through the infected mother to her baby during pregnancy, birth, or breast-feeding.

So in the chart, there is a dark Moon rising. It is not a reference to Lilith or anything like that, but it is a dark Moon rising. It is a potentially lethal Moon rising. It is ruled by Mars and Pluto, which are going into Libra, into the 12th House. Again, the idea of the secret enemy. And then that rulership goes right on up here to Venus conjunct the North Node in the zodiac sign of Cancer, which is connected to mother and to nurturing. Venus in Cancer is then ruled by the Moon, which then reappears at the rising point of the astrological chart. So what you have there is a kind of tight circuit where you've got the rulers of Scorpio going into the 12th, going up to the Venus, which is then ruled by the Moon which is rising. So basically, in my mind, this was hitting all of those particular points which were descriptive of the virus. Out of this comes the red ribbon, which is right now rather iconic for ACT UP, which was the protest "Silence = Death" at the beginning of the lecture; that is their motto, which was to open up the eyes and ears of the medical establishment.

This is Diana (Image 12), goddess of the Moon, the older sister of Apollo, in fact, after she's born she turns around and helps give birth to Apollo. Diana is also connected with arrows, bows and arrows. And here she is both the protector and the slayer of young women. Hera, who doesn't like Diana very much, says to her, "A lion to women Zeus has made you, to kill any at your pleasure."

Image 12: Diana, Goddess of the Moon

Women who died in childbirth were direct victims of Diana. So just as Apollo is the healing god and a plague god, Diana's presence is known from the piercing cry of the woman in childbirth, because the piercing cry comes from being shot with arrows by Diana. She came to her to give her release, but was the release going to be the birth of a child, or was the release going to be in death? Okay, so this ambiguity exists with Diana and it exists with the Moon. And what I found interesting, as a side note, was the alliance over a period of time—though it was never really a formal one—but this kind of coming together of the breast cancer movement and the ACT UP movement, the common ground being to form a political voice to force the government to speed up approval of medications to make them available and not to sit on them. And what I just found interesting as a side note is that Nancy Brinker founded the Komen Foundation, which fought to bring awareness to breast cancer, founded it in honor of her sister in 1982, the same year as the appearance of the AIDS chart.

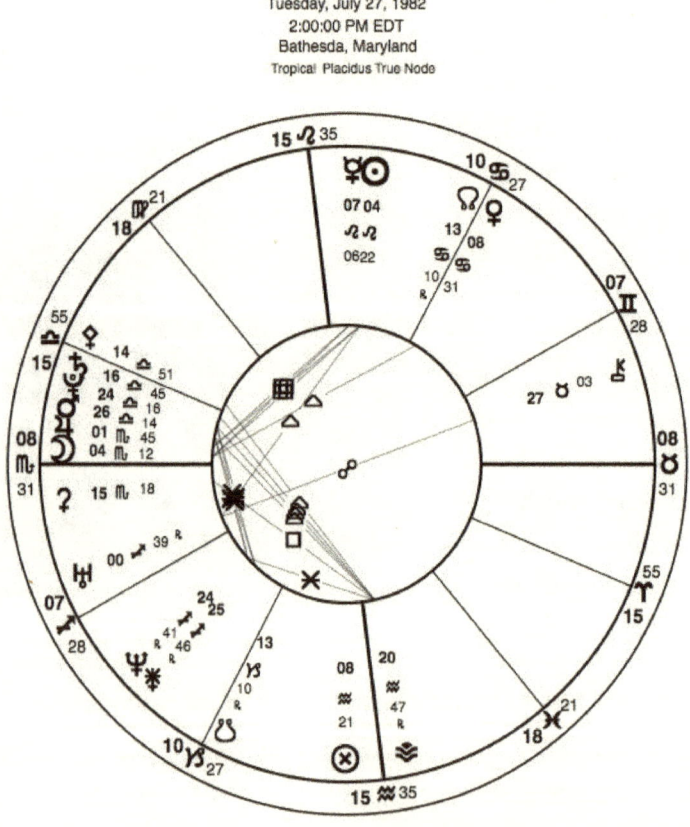

Image 13: AIDS Virus Chart

Now, I'd like to continue. This one is a little funky, but there was just something about the imagery that I couldn't resist. But I actually do want to hit this other idea now.

This Moon, Mars, and Pluto conjunct in Libra ruled by Venus, in my opinion, is kind of the main action of the chart. It spoke to me of perhaps the possibility that the AIDS virus could be a chronic condition, a manageable condition, rather than one that would be fatal. At that time it was fatal. But this is the life-span of the chart.

This is AIDS's chart, theoretically. And so for me what I found fascinating was the trine. We're used to talking about the trine as being a harmonizing or facilitating energy—people kind of even make fun of it and say it makes you complacent or lazy and things like that, and perhaps that's what it does—but, and this is completely anecdotal, in the work that I've done as an astrologer, I also find that trines act as protection. They only show up if you need it. So there's a mixed idea there. At first it's like, "Wow! That's a trine! That's good!" But it is also protection. Well, why do you need protection? Because you are being threatened, or there is something that wants to take away what would be your good fortune. So the idea of this facilitating energy and protection was something that just kind of popped out at me. And it got me thinking: Could the appearance of this trine suggest that AIDS might not be just a death sentence? And then because Judith Hill swears by this book, I looked it up in Cornell's reference on chronic diseases. H. L. Cornell writes in *Encyclopedia of Medical Astrology*:

> ...In Greek mythology, Saturn is called Chronos, from which our word chronic is taken. The 12th House and Saturn—bear in mind that Saturn is in its Joy in the 12th House—the Sun is in its Joy in the 9th House, Saturn is in its Joy in the 12th House. The 12th House and Saturn have general rule over chronic diseases and those which tend to become morbid. While permanent diseases proceed from Saturn, their course is regulated by the motion of the Sun, and it is very essential to watch the

aspects to or afflictions to the Sun to give a prognosis or forecast concerning the probable outcome of a chronic disease. (p. 106)

And so I thought it was also very interesting that the Sun is moving into sextile to Saturn, which is there in its Joy.

Now for the funky part. I have a confession to make, which is I have only recently started working with asteroids. Don't hate me, because I wasn't quite sure, like, whatever, I'm a Capricorn, and we're just stodgy old fucks. But anyway, gradually

Image 14: Chiron the Centaur

we come around to the idea. And so this is why it is funky. But what I found interesting—and if you were at Chani's talk earlier she brought up Chiron at this degree, which is 27—it happened to appear in the chart of the poetess (Audre Lorde). It also happens to appear in this chart, and so Chiron is conjunct Algol, which we know is a binary star and is connected to Medusa.

Algol is at 25⁰ Taurus at this time, and Chiron is at 27⁰ Taurus. And according to Diana Rosenberg in her book *Secrets of the Ancient Skies*, "Algol often marks great tragedies, the sort of events in which many die or are killed brutally. It is remarkable that the Chinese found this area extremely hateful as well. To them, Algol was Tseih She, which meant 'the heaped up corpses,' central star of Tal-ing, the great trench, a mass grave of piled-up, deliberately dishonored and dismembered remains"

Image 15: Perseus and Algol

(Rosenberg, p. 200-201). The fixed stars which align close to that are the Pleiades, which is a star cluster.

Pleiades was connected to the weeping sisters, and according to Anthony Lewis in H*orary Astrology Plain and Simple*, this is connected to the weeping sisters so it always means something to cry about, unlucky, exile, suffering, so it's this idea again. What I find also interesting, I came across this on Marina Partridge's website (darkstarastrology.com, it's a great site), and what she also pointed out is that the Pleiades, according to Manilius, they might have been the weeping sisters, but, Manilius says, "at the emergence of his back rising with his head hanging down, the bull brings forth in his 6th degree (it was the 6th degree when Manilius was writing in Rome) the Pleiades, sisters who vie with each other's radiance." So, instead of weeping sisters all of a sudden we are getting sisters vying with each other's radiance. You know, a little bitchy. Manilius writes:

Beneath their influence, devotees of Bacchus and Venus are born into the kindly light, and people whose insouciance—which means a "devil-may-care, cavalier, casual, what's-it-mean-to-me?" attitude—people whose insouciance runs free at feasts and banquets and who strive to provoke sweet mirth with biting wit. They will always take pains over personal adornment and an elegant appearance. They will set their locks in waves of curls or confine their tresses with bands,

Image 16: 1980s Drag Queens

building them into a thick topknot (perhaps you remember the topknot that Apollo was also brandishing) – a thick topknot, and they will transform the appearance of the head by adding hair to it. They will smooth their hairy limbs with the porous pumice, loathing their manhood and craving for sleekness of arm. They adopt feminine dress, footwear donned not for wear but for show, and an affected effeminate gait. They are ashamed of their sex. In their hearts dwells a senseless passion for display, and they boast of their malady, which they call a virtue. To give their love is never enough, they will also want their love to be seen (Manilius, p. 313).

Now, if that wasn't a Roman description of a drag queen, I don't know what is!

So the idea of Chiron is the wounded healer. Are we all generally familiar with the myth of Chiron? He is the son of Apollo. He is half-human, half-mortal; half-human, half-horse. Like Apollo, Chiron hangs out with boys. You don't really see him teaching the healing arts to girls. Chiron is teaching Achilles and Hercules sword play and how to be manly men. And he's teaching Asclepius how to heal. So his company is, again, young men; again the Ephebes are in that age group. Chiron is seen as the most civilized of the centaurs. He mirrors Apollo with arts and sciences, with his ability to heal, and to teach astrology, which was also something that was connected to him. And at this really bad wedding party, and the centaurs were always the party animals, they were always the ones you questioned, "Do you really want them at the wedding?" And so they would show up and get horsey! You know, horse play. They drank too much and they were always doing things like running away with the bridesmaids, and the bride, abducting them, having their way and a wild time. And so this is what happened at this party. Everything went wrong. So Hercules takes the bow and arrow–that theme again–and he shoots it and basically wipes out every single centaur for this particular tribe. Someone once asked me in one of my classes what happened to the bride and the bridesmaids? We don't know! The centaurs were wiped out, but Chiron was wounded. And so he was wounded with the blood of the Hydra. It could not be healed.

Chiron becomes this dichotomy of the wounded healer. What's interesting is also the idea that—and it comes from the myth of Telephos, who is the king of Mezia, who was also wounded by Achilles—it won't heal. He goes to the oracle to ask what he could do to heal his wound, and the oracle says, "The wounder heals." So, Chiron is the wounded healer, but yet there's this connection to this idea that the wounder himself heals. And if you practice homeopathy you're going to be familiar to some extent with introducing something that's toxic is the very thing that's going to heal. But that also sets up this double play idea that the person who is healing sends the plague. You know, the person who wounded is also the person you have to go to for healing. And indeed Achilles, who had speared this king, rubs rust off of his spear and so the king is saved.

Chiron is this idea of living with terminal pain. But there is a part of the myth that also stayed with me, and that is how the myth ends. Chiron is half mortal, half immortal. He is in so much agony that there is this deal that is being worked out between Zeus and Prometheus. Prometheus is bound and his liver is being eaten every day by an eagle because he brought fire to men, which is its own story, but there is this deal that Mercury or Hermes and Zeus are negotiating. Zeus says to him, "Prometheus can go free, if you have someone to take his place." So, Chiron volunteers to take the place of Prometheus. But, taking the place of Prometheus, for Chiron, means that he's going to die because unlike Prometheus, Chiron's liver won't regrow after it's been devoured. Prometheus was an immortal. His liver, devoured by the eagle, would naturally regrow. This was not the case with Chiron. When the eagle comes to devour Chiron's liver, he kills Chiron in what must have been an agonizing death. Chiron is a god who dies because he is only half immortal. Chiron is not a salvation figure. A wound can be healed, but the body will ultimately deteriorate. Moreover Chiron is a myth that deals with euthanasia as well as suicide and assisted suicide. This was quite prevalent in the 1980s and early 1990s given the fatal prognosis of AIDS.

Image 17: AIDS Quilt at the Washington DC Mall

So here we have the idea of heaping up of bodies, the weeping sisters, the drag queen or vying sisters, and this idea of this wound–this incurable wound. And so, to me, the AIDS quilt in Washington represents all of those ideas.

The idea of the heaping up of bodies, the way that it is being displayed and put out in front of the polis, in front of the government, for people to see. And again, just even looking at the photograph, there are no words. There's no speech. "Silence = Death," and here is the silent testament to what is going on at the time.

So these degrees–these 27, 25, 29 degrees–stayed with me. And I found them again in this horoscope, which is the Robert Rayford death chart.

Robert Rayford is the first AIDS fatality, a light-skinned African-American boy, who was sixteen when he died of the virus on May 15, 1969. This is his death chart. In Missouri. And nobody knew about AIDS at the time. It was a doctor who had been tending to him. When she was reading about the opportunistic infections that were showing up with people suffering from AIDS in the 1980s, she went back to Robert Rayford's blood sample that they had kept frozen and they tested it, and he tested positive for the AIDS virus. So its appearance in the country was before when people had thought it showed up. There is a Sun-Moon conjunction here at 23^0 and 25^0 Taurus.

Audience: How did he get it?

Christopher: That's the big question. He spoke very little. He hardly said a word. And he would show up for regular testing for months. And the only thing that he really shared was, "Well, they call me quite a stud." And so what was suspected was that he was a hustler, a street hustler. That's all they know of his background.

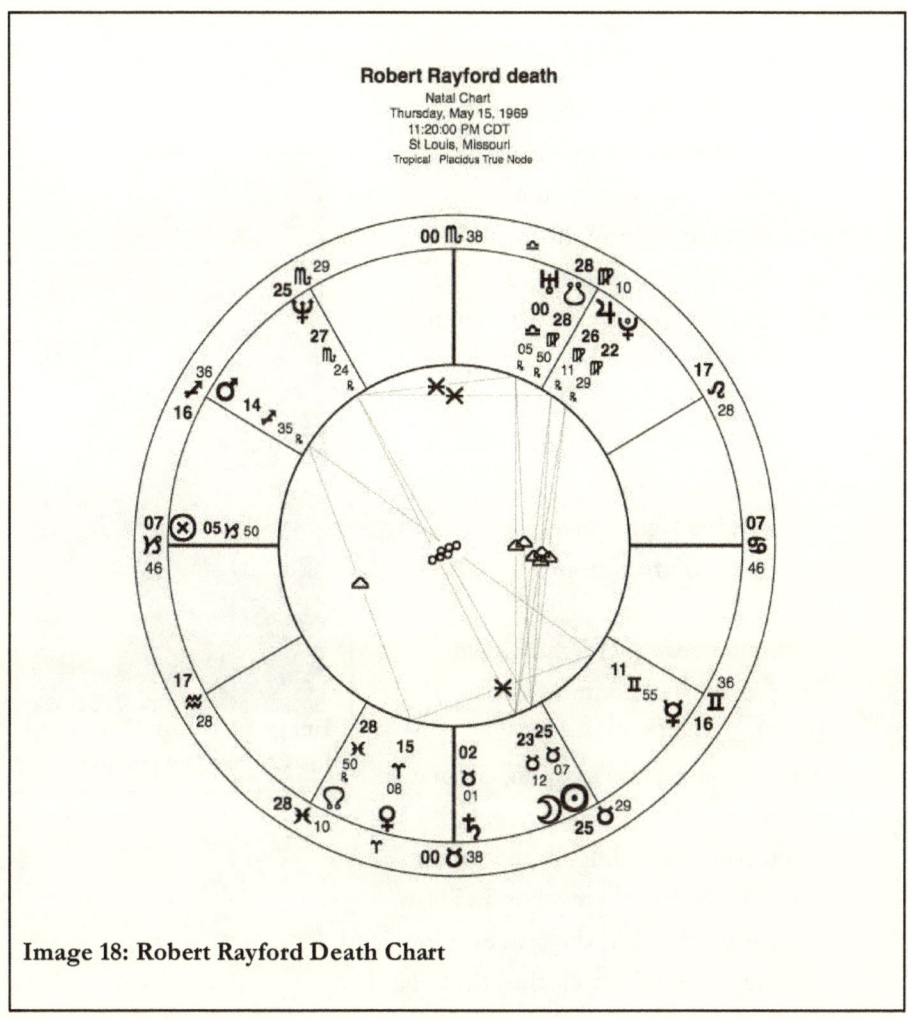

Image 18: Robert Rayford Death Chart

But what I find fascinating is this idea: It is not quite the New Moon, the Moon is heading towards the Sun, and so it is almost like it is dropping a seed into fallow ground. So I'm not going to say, oh, I know what this means, I don't. I just find it a really fascinating piece of sky, what is going on in these charts, and what it is connecting.

OK, Saturn. The Saturn return of AIDS. Saturn is in its Joy in the 12th House, and it is exalted in Libra.

> Saturn is my name
> I'm first of planets, high above the earth.
> I am by nature dry and cold,
> And my works are manifold.
> I in my houses firmly stand–
> The Goat and the Waterman.
> I do much damage by my might,
> On sea and land, by day and night.
> My exaltation's in the Scales,
> But in the Ram my power fails.
> It's thirty years, harsh and malign,
> Ere I come again
> to the same sign.
> My children are vicious,
> dry and old,
> Envious, weary, wretched, cold.
> Deep eyes, hard skin,
> their beards small.
> They're lame, misshapen, depraved withal.
> Traitorous, brooding, greedy, pale,
> They often find themselves in jail.
> They grub the dirt, dig graves, plow land,
> In foul and stinking clothes they stand.
> Condemned to die or live in sorrow,
> Sweat and strain, or trouble borrow,
> Always needy, never free,
> It's Saturn's children there you see.

Image 19: Saturn Devouring his Children by Goya

Image 20: **Saturn and His Children**

Unapologetic! The way that I work with the Saturn return is the same way that I work with the lunar cycles. The first quarter is waxing, it's building. When it's opposite its placement, at its culmination, it starts to fade. The third angle is when it's waning, it's fading. And then the return is the new message or, with the AIDS crisis, where are we now with this. So, I went to the first quarter, working with roughly seven to seven-and-a-half years, but I went to the first quarter, and I found that on August 18, 1990, when Saturn is basically squaring the Saturn in the AIDS chart, Saturn is at 19^0 Capricorn, so it's squaring the Saturn at 16^0 Libra.

On August 18, 1990, the Ryan White Care Act was passed. And that was the first time there was any action taken on the part of government to do something for people who were afflicted or suffering from HIV. Ryan White died earlier that year of AIDS on April 8, 1990, when Saturn was at 24^0 Capricorn.

Image 21: **Ryan White**

Ryan White died at the age of eighteen, again, another teenager. The boy who was the first AIDS victim is a teenager, and here you have Ryan White, a young boy who becomes, really, the poster child of doing something merciful, something to help out people who are facing this illness. Ronald Reagan–the reason why you see him on that AIDSGate poster–refused to say the word AIDS out loud. He wouldn't say it. And so there was the question, "People are dying, Mr. President, will you say something?" And that first quarter, up to 1990, was hideous. You had Jesse Helms, who was amending a federal appropriation bill that prohibited AIDS education. You could not speak of homosexual activity in schools. There's William F. Buckley in the *New York Times* article, who called for mandatory testing of HIV and said that any HIV gay men should have this information forcibly tattooed on their buttocks. And HIV drug users should be tattooed on their arms. There's a famous incident, which I read about in "The Truth about Reagan and AIDS" by Michael Bronski, in which he says, "the most memorable Reagan AIDS moment was at the 1986 Centenary rededication of the Statue of Liberty. The Reagans were there, sitting next to the French prime minister and his wife, François and Danielle Mitterrand. Bob Hope was on stage, entertaining the all-star audience. In the middle of a series of one-liners, Hope quipped, 'I just heard that the Statue of Liberty has AIDS, but she doesn't know if she got it from the mouth of the Hudson, or the Staten Island Ferry.' As the television camera panned the audience, the Mitterands looked appalled; the Reagans were laughing."

Image 22: AIDSGate Poster

By the end of 1989, 115,786 women and men had been diagnosed with AIDS in the United States and more than 70,000 of them had died. The reason why Ryan White is so important is that he was a child with hemophilia, and his school would not allow him to attend. He had to take his lessons over the phone. He brought this to court and he won, and the response was for him to be hazed and harassed to the point where they had to switch to another school. So he basically became the face of all of that.

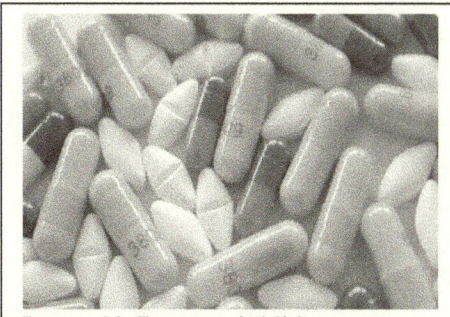
Image 23: Protease inhibitors

The fourteenth year, which is when Saturn is opposite the Saturn in the AIDS chart, at this point it is at 6^0 Aries and Mars is at 3^0 Libra retrograde. Mars is actually returning to Libra at this point, and Saturn is opposite at 3^0 Aries on February 27, 1997, and that is when it was announced by the CDC they had documented the first ever decline in AIDS deaths in the United States of America. So Saturn had reached its opposition and was starting to lose its energy, and that is the first time when the body count comes down. And that is a direct result of the anti-retrovirals, or the protease inhibitors which were being made available at that time.

Image 24: Bill Clinton

And so we come to this fellow, Bill Clinton, for our twenty-first year, who again is a mixed figure. He connects to our story through "Don't Ask, Don't Tell." We continue with the non-communication theme. I don't think it's a coincidence that Clinton is a Leo in contrast to Reagan the Aquarius, that there is this diametric opposition in signs between the two gentlemen. On October 23, 2003–this marks about twenty-one years–the William J. Clinton Foundation secured price reductions for HIV/AIDS drugs for generic manufacturers to benefit developing nations. Saturn is at 13° Cancer. So building on the momentum of this, you have the medication being made available

Again, when you reflect on the 9th House, long journeys, foreign countries, worldly travel…plagues, famously, as Susan Sontag points out in *AIDS and Its Metaphors*, were seen as "foreign born." They came from foreign countries like the ship in Marseilles, the plague that comes from the east. So a plague was not something that was native born. It was foreign. It came through immigrants. It came through people who were trying to come into your country to ruin it. So that idea of foreign travel and other locations are also connected to the 9th House.

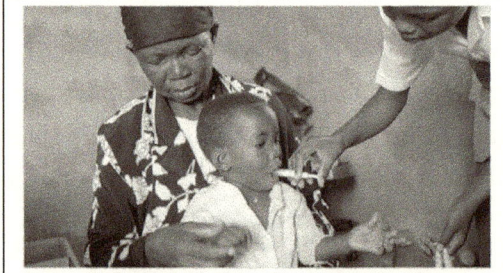
Image 25: HIV Meds Being Distributed in Africa

The Saturn Return chart that I find compelling takes place on August 4, 2010. Again, it's in the month of Leo. I don't quite pretend to understand the relationship here other than it is interestingly coincidental. But on August 4, 2010, Judge Vaughn Walker overturned Proposition 8. Libra–Saturn is in Libra–is the zodiac sign of the law, the sign of the scales of justice, as well as the zodiac sign of marriage. What makes a marriage a marriage is the legal document that recognizes the spousal relationship between two adults. In his ruling, Judge Walker ruled that, "Proposition 8 fails to advance any rational basis in singling out gay men and lesbians for denial of a marriage license. Indeed, Proposition 8 does nothing more than enshrine in the California constitution that opposite-sex couples are superior to same-sex couples, because Proposition 8 prevents California from fulfilling its constitutional obligation to provide marriages on an equal basis. The Court concluded that Proposition 8 was

Image 26: Judge Vaughn Walker

unconstitutional." And this takes place on August 4, 2010, when Saturn is at 1^0 Libra, and Mars happens to be in Libra at the same time. It's at 3^0 Libra. So, the two planets have returned together.

Audience: In the natal chart you have for AIDS, the Mars has been in Libra for seven months at that point, it's been doing its retrograding in Libra; and then at the Saturn-Saturn opposition in '97, we start to see the decrease for the first time, that's the next Mars retrograde in Libra. And then the next Mars retrograde in Libra is next spring. So there's a pattern. It's a Mars-ruled chart, Scorpio Rising.

Christopher: Right, thank you for noticing that. So essentially what we have here is we start out with funerals and we end with weddings. What does that mean? Saturn is exalted in Libra. Does that mean Saturn's on its best behavior? Or Saturn really gets to rip you a new one? What do these terminologies mean?

Image 27: Just Married

I just got married. *(Applause)* I like this image. It shows the change from youth into maturity. How I interpret this is that the next step for the gay community is, okay, are you going to step up to the plate and take a place in society? And what does that mean to you? Marriage isn't just a heterosexual tradition. It's also regarded—and this came up in a lot of the Supreme Court arguments—as providing a cornerstone to society. The idea that, in fact, what was being voiced was, do not make it heterosexist. Make it so that people can marry, that by bonding and by harmonizing and by creating alliances, this creates stronger society, at least theoretically speaking. I mean just because I'm married doesn't mean I'm going to start saying, "Oh marriage is great." I've been with my husband for twenty years, but the thing is, what you have here is moving from the margin or the youthful or the outcast or the downtrodden into a place where you are going to participate in society.

So how are you going to participate in this society? How are you going to mold or influence the society? At the end of the Watkins report, which came out in 1988 and was submitted to the President of the United States, there was a suggestion to change policy about medications. Watkins writes, "A society is judged by how it responds to those in greatest need. A tragedy such as the HIV epidemic brings a society face to face with the core of its established values, and offers an opportunity for the re-affirmation of compassion, justice, and dignity." And so by stepping up and taking the place in the polis—which I think is basically how we can interpret this Saturn return—we raise these new questions.

The journey of Saturn through the signs has transformed the gay population, it has brought it into the mainstream. Gays may even become the working model for marriage. I don't know how many people read *The Atlantic Monthly*, or subscribe to it, but that's what was on the cover. Basically, "What can gays teach straights, or queers teach straights, about marriage?" And it's a very lengthy article saying this is your new guidebook.

Okay, there's something that's going on here. It transformed health care. People can no longer be turned down for pre-existing conditions. There is outreach to Africa and to other nations that are struggling with the disease. It transformed sex, because it certainly introduced the idea of safe sex and responsibility and accountability.

And finally, what I see in this—the dialogue which is just beginning—the concept of the right to die. What do you do if your illness is incurable? Saturn in Scorpio. To me, Saturn is always bringing out the taboos that are connected to that sign. What is one of the greatest taboos that we still face? Suicide. Do you have the right to take your own life? And how will that be set up or framed? All of these things I see as coming out of this dialogue.

The last picture is of my late partner, Brian Greenbaum, and then I'll take questions. He would have loved this world and what we have.

Cherish what you have. You fought hard for it. You've lived hard for it. You've loved hard for it. See it as a wonderful thing that you bring to the table, to your community, to your city, to your government, and to your world. Thank you.

Image 28: Brian Greenbaum

References

Bronski, M. (2004). "The Truth about Reagan and AIDS." *Z Magazine*. http://zcomm.org/zmagazine/the-truth-about-reagan-and-aids-by-michael-bronski/

Cornell, H. L. (1972). *Encyclopedia of Medical Astrology*. Samuel Weiser, Inc.

Evatt, B. L. (2006). "The Tragic History of AIDS in the Hemophilia Population 1982-1984." J Thromb Haemost. 4 (22). 95-301.

Hansen, M. (2000). "The Planets and their Children: A Blockbook of Medieval Popular Astrology." Accessed on website: http://www.billyandcharlie.com/planets/

Houlding, D. (2006). *The Houses: Temples of the Sky*. The Wessex Astrologer Ltd.

Manilius, M. (1908). *Astronomica*. Weicher.

Mass, Lawrence MD. (1989). "Medical answers about AIDS." Created and distributed by the New York City Department of Health and Gay Men's Health Crisis, Inc.

"The Watkins Report." (1988). President's Commission on the HIV Epidemic.

Sontag, S. (1989). *AIDS and its Metaphors* (1st ed.). New York: Farrar, Straus and Giroux.

Images

Image 6. Marginal Waters #9. (1985). Doug Ischar. Appears courtesy of the artist.

Image 8. Ken Meeks with KS. © Alon Reininger/(Contact Press Images)

Myths of Gender, Gender in Myth: Queering Astrology with Mythology

Rhea Wolf

As we approach, question, and cultivate a Queer Astrology, we are invited to see not only relationships outside of a mainstream, heteronormative view, but also the individual. Queering astrology requires us to go beyond our assumptions, past experiences, cookbook description and labels, in order to instead see the person in front of us—whether the self, a friend or a client. Relationships are key in unlocking some of the stereotypical language in the astrological canon, but it is not only in viewing and interpreting relationship patterns that we need to look through a queer lens. Understanding the relationships between different parts of ourselves is vital as well.

First, some definitions of queer:

1. strange; odd (Oxford American Dictionary)
2. differing in some odd way from what is usual or normal (Merriam-Webster Dictionary)
3. *often disparaging:* homosexual (Merriam-Webster Dictionary)
4. Think of queer as an umbrella term. It includes anyone who a) wants to identify as queer and b) who feels somehow outside of the societal norms in regards to gender, sexuality or/and even politics. (PFLAG website)

Here's my definition: Anyone committed to knowing who they are in all their parts without relying on stereotypical, pre-assigned, or socially acceptable notions of gender, sexuality, relationships, time, and space. To be queer is to be open to the moment. To be queer is to look at things differently than you've been told to. To be queer is to inhabit a different time and space than the homogenous, heteronormative, consumer culture. To be queer is to focus on the process of creating a life rather than on producing labels, constructing ideologies or manufacturing stability.

Now, I'd like to bring in a word that I feel is closely related to queer and the reclamation of identity back from cultural, familial, or political agendas.

Query:

1. a question, esp. one addressed to an official or organization
2. to ask a question about something, esp. in order to express one's doubts about it or to check its validity or accuracy
3. a doubt in the mind; a mental reservation

(from *The Merriam-Webster Dictionary* and *The Free Dictionary*)

Similarly, *queering* something means leaning into the questions, allowing uncertainty and unknowing, moving beyond our expectations so that something new can emerge. We may query our gender, social status, or political choices in order to see if they are valid and accurate representations of who we feel ourselves to be.

An astrology that doesn't liberate is not interesting to me. That goes for the personal as well as the societal level. At this moment in astrology's history, perhaps more than any other time, we are at a crossroads. We have very recently learned much more about our past than we previously knew. We are also reaching a level of maturation in terms of the psychological and innovative techniques of the twentieth century. All of this has the capacity to create a lot of confusion as well as positive re-imagining. We don't quite know what is happening. But it seems like the time is ripe to generate an astrology of liberation that includes rather than excludes, that empowers rather than rejects, that expands the possible rather than narrowly defining reality.

Since we are dealing with a system that originated thousands of years ago, there are of course many rules, techniques, practices and schools of thought about the art and science of astrology. The methodology has been practiced, observed and revised time and again. And although there are many things about astrology that we may consider to be unimpeachable, sometimes it seems like each of us practices in our own unique way. We often joke at these conferences that when you get a bunch of astrologers in the same room, no one can agree on the best house system, etc. What I'm saying is that there are ways that ancient and even modern uses of astrological language will feel at odds with the energy of inclusivity and specificity that queer and feminist language requires. By playing with the language and entertaining changes, I feel that rather than losing the accuracy and precision of astrological delineation, we will uncover better ways of understanding and supporting people.

As we queer astrology, we are really cultivating resiliency, fluidity and a relationship with uncertainty as we update our astrological language.
For Queer Astrology to come into its own, we have to move beyond 7th House couplism and duality. Let's face it, the 7th House was originally about contracts. Literally, the patriarch gives money and security, and the wife provides the heirs. Contracts can be useful, but do they really tell us anything about the two people within the arrangement or describe how these two might otherwise see and cherish each other? Queer relationships are about whole people seeing one another for who they are, daring to go outside of societal expectations or economic arrangements.

In my practice, the use of mythological figures has often helped illuminate the circumstances, challenges, and potentials of current transits for my clients. Rather than being penned into mundane, conventional versions of self, identifying with a myth can raise our awareness of self to another level, invite questions, and further us on our individual quests.

Even in the beginning of my studies of astrology, I was dissatisfied with binary gender language which ascribed certain planets to certain people based on their biological sex. Like: in a woman's chart, Mars will indicate the kind of man she will be attracted to or the kind of man she attracts. It just felt wrong. As a queer woman, a feminist and a witch, I am rarely satisfied with the way things are supposed to be.

Regardless of my sexual orientation or gender status, I'm very capable of having Mars energy in my own damn right. I mean, the Natal Chart is MY natal chart, so everything in it is about me: how I behave, how I think, how I perceive the world, how others perceive me. Mars or Venus isn't about the one man or one woman I was searching so desperately for. The Sun and the Moon do not have total domain over our experiences of the father or mother, Venus does not accurately describe my role as a woman…there were definitely short-comings in the mid-20th century astrological language.

Anytime I read texts from the ancient astrological libraries, I feel like I have to stand on my head in order to decode what the fuck they were talking about. I mean, in terms of gender, class, race, etc., especially when so many planets are given a masculine orientation, often based upon the gods associated with the planet.

When I discovered the Asteroid Goddesses in the form of Demetra George's work, I was elated. Here were the feminine planets that would reflect more accurately my life experiences and values. I poured over the major ones like Vesta and Ceres and reached out to learn the names, if not the astrological attributes, of other lesser known ones, such as Psyche, Iris, and Daphne. I had already been using mythology as a main component of my practice, and the increase in information about asteroids enriched my work with clients.

> **Signs Classified by Gender**
>
> **Feminine (Earth and Water)**
> Taurus, Cancer, Virgo, Scorpio, Capricorn, Pisces
>
> **Masculine (Fire and Air)**
> Aries, Gemini, Leo, Libra, Sagittarius, Aquarius

Here's where it gets tricky: I actually like simplicity. I love that we have the option to look at millions of asteroids, dwarf planets, centaurs, and planetoids. But it can be overwhelming. I didn't necessarily want to have to look at so-called minor astronomical bodies to find representations of the feminine. So even with all of these heavenly objects to look upon, there was still something missing. Again, it felt funky to me that the major planets were mostly masculine gender-identified and related to male gods in most of the cultures that practiced astrology.

> **The Dual Rulerships of Planets**
>
> **Mercury:** Gemini and Virgo
>
> **Venus:** Taurus and Libra
>
> **Mars:** Aries and Scorpio
>
> **Jupiter:** Sagittarius and Pisces
>
> **Saturn:** Capricorn and Aquarius

It was actually when I went back to the ancient roots of astrological lineage that I was able to find insight into the modern, changing perception of gender and how I could tease out more fluid and accurate representations within mythological and astrological discussion.

A light bulb went off when I began seriously working with ancient rulerships, in which each of the seven visible planets, excepting the Moon and Sun, were the rulers of two signs apiece.

And of these signs, one was invariably of the masculine gender while the other was of the feminine gender. This may still seem like we are working on the binary gender system, and we are. But it broke up the masculine domination of the planets. At least for me. All of a sudden Mars was the ruler of Aries, a masculine sign, and Scorpio, a feminine sign.

Planetary Domiciles

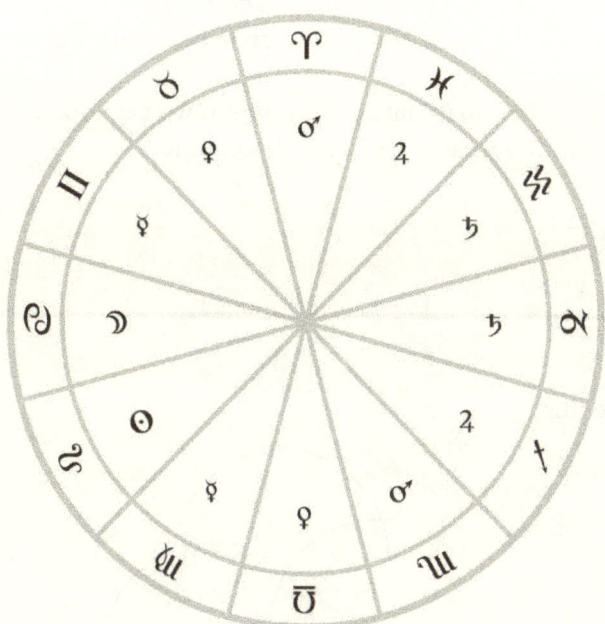

I still love the asteroids and the newly named dwarf planets like Eris and Sedna. I think they have something immensely valuable to add to our understanding of the universe as well as the nature of archetypes within human consciousness. But I have been excited to break apart and examine the ways that Mars, often associated with the Roman god of war, is feminine.

Now looking at the planets in this way is not revolutionary, but it can help break apart ways of thinking about gender, sexuality and the planets. Rulerships help me find new stories, myths, folktales, and pop culture references that symbolize the planetary energies.

As astrologers, we have a big responsibility to use discipline and discernment in our language anytime we meet with a client. When working with clients that identify as genderqueer or transgender, this responsibility is amplified.

For me, working on this continuum between the feminine and masculine archetypes is really about allowing the full spectrum of shades in between. This is how the binary system is helpful, as extreme points of view that help us facilitate an understanding of everything else. It's the same way that the religious right's extreme stances on things like women's rights, gay marriage, and abortion might actually help mainstream Americans become more moderate and considered. The extremes show us a pure form of an archetype, or the caricature of that pure form.

But beyond the binary linear continuum, we can look at the spheres of energies as they interact, overlap and combine.

Rather than this:

We can have this:

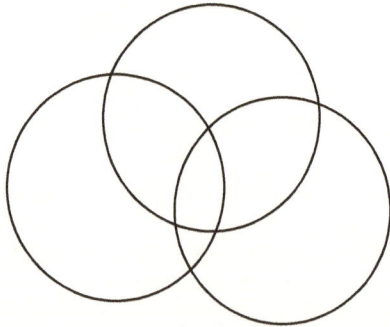

As opposed to the line, which gives us only variations along a continuum, seeing gender, for example, as an interlocking set of qualities, presentations, desires, etc. gives us a much more interesting and complex way of expressing who we are.

This way of looking at gender, the planets, or a personal natal chart reminds me of what Carl Jung would say before listening to someone recall a dream. "I have no idea what this means," he would say to himself.

I still find a lot of frustration with how the use of archetypes and astrology still follows such a narrowly defined gender system. But for me, as I said, this way of playing with the planets and gender helps me see the stories and themes, the strengths and challenges that a person may be dealing with, rather than focusing on their perceived or presented gender in order to make predictions and evaluations. Polarities are all over the place in astrology, and in life itself. And they do have something to teach us, as I've said. Tension is often necessary before a breakthrough happens.

Definitions of polarity

1. the separation, alignment or orientation of something into two opposed poles
2. either of the two extremes of such attributes

Examples of polarity beyond binary gender

Inhale – exhale ♦ rhythm – melody ♦ positive – negative
slow – fast ♦ activity – rest ♦ work – home
candor – diplomacy ♦ gentle – tough ♦ form – formlessness
holding – releasing ♦ motion – stillness

But beyond polarity, which often asks us to consider only two opposing forces, how can we instead look for resonances as we consider the planets presenting themselves to us in a variety of flavors?

An article titled "The Queer Craft" explores queer experience in pagan circles. From his experiences as a gay man practicing witchcraft,

Storm Faerywolf writes about polarities and the perception of gender as opposite:

> My own experience has shown me that as a gay man I exist outside the parameters of "normal" society...I represented something "Other" that could at times encompass traits usually described as masculine or feminine but also had qualities that were beyond the normal limits of both. The Yin/Yang model doesn't accurately describe the Universe in its entirety, just as the God/Goddess model fails to do the same. These are maps and metaphors that we have set into place in an attempt to have a relationship to the cosmos at large, but we should understand that these models themselves cannot completely define the Universe. No model ever could.[1]

To create space for a queer astrology, it demands that we be flexible and open to surprise. Maybe we cannot ever truly be free of our own biases and perceptions based on experience, but we can undertake a journey as astrologers to help us understand those biases so that we are less vulnerable to being blinded by them.

One of the primary ways I practice astrology with clients is to look at the mythic energies trying to be released in the planetary positions and current transits.

Here, I am including a list of different deities for exploration. Gods and Goddesses are not bound by gender in their presentation, nor are they always human in form. I find that when we place real life circumstances within the context of a mythological tale, attitudes, issues, biases and fears around gender can begin to dissipate.

---

1. Faerywolf, S. (2000). The queer craft: Rethinking magickal polarity. http://faerywolf.com/queer-craft/

For Further Exploration: Deities and Planetary Energies

The names which follow here do not necessarily correspond to the planetary rulers that were specific to a given culture. They are listed according to thematic or mythological affinity. Let yourself explore their stories to see how these gods and goddesses bring varying examples of how a planet might present itself in life.

Sun: Amaterasu (Japanese), Apollo (Greek), Sol (Germanic), Sula (Celtic), Inanna (Sumerian), Bast (Egyptian), Ra (Egyptian), Gnowee (Aboriginal)

Moon: Selene (Greek), Hina (Polynesian), Sin (Mesopotamian), Arianrhod (Celtic), Yemaya (Yoruba), Anningan (Inuit), Tsukuyomi (Japanese). Mawu/Lisa *is a Sun/Moon deity of the Fon People of West Africa.*

Mercury: Hermes (Greek), Thoth (Egyptian), Ninshubur (Sumerian), Iris (Greek), Coyote (North American), Loki (Norse), Brigid (Celtic), Papa Legba (Haitian Vodou)

Venus: Aphrodite (Greek), Freya (Norse), Dion y glas (Feri), Krishna (Hindu), Shukra (Hindu), The Green Man (various), Eros (Greek)

Mars: Ares (Greek), Artemis (Greek), Xena (The Cult of Lucy Lawless), Boudica (Irish), Amazons (Greek), Sekhmet (Egyptian), Athena (Greek), Buffy Summers (The Universe of Joss Whedon)

Jupiter: Lakshmi (Hindu), Dionysus (Greek), Zeus (Greek), Taranis (Celtic), Hathor (Egyptian), Yahweh or Jehovah (Judeo-Christian), Yemaya (Yoruba)

Saturn: The Fates (Greek), The Norns (Norse), Demeter (Greek), Set (Egyptian), Chronos (Greek), Mother Holle (German), Psyche (Greek), Cernunnos (Celtic), Hera (Greek)

Uranus: Ix Chel (Maya), Prometheus (Greek), Horus (Egyptian), Odin (Norse), Daedalus (Greek), The Djinn (Islam), Jesus (Christian), Cybele (Phrygian)

Neptune: Mary (Christian), Manannán mac Lir (Irish), Amphitrite (Greek), Poseidon (Greek), Tiamat (Mesopotamian), Leviathan (Judeo-Christian)

Pluto: Kali (Hindu), Hades (Greek), Erishkigal (Sumerian), Hecate (Greek), Osiris (Egyptian), The Morrigan (Celtic), Persephone (Greek), Hel (Norse), Shiva (Hindu), Pele (Hawaiian)

Ideas and questions for discussion:

- Could identifying mythological representations of the planets help you see beyond gender? Is it still too limiting for you? What are other ways to imagine and embody the energy of the planets?

- How do you imagine your own gender? Write about this. Finish the sentence: "When I think about how gender and sexuality affect my life, I feel…"

- What are some helpful things that astrology does in relation to the question of gender identity and otherwise? Write about it: "The ways astrology has supported my identity are…"

- What do we want to see change in our astrological canon? Write it out: "If I had my way, astrology would include…"

- What are some examples of how astrology has hindered or repressed your authentic experience of your gender identity?

Queer Talk on Client Work

Barry Perlman and Jessica Lanyadoo

Jessica Lanyadoo and Barry Perlman presenting at the Queer Astrology Conference, 2013. Photo by Luciano Sagastume.

BARRY: I'm Barry. I always like to start off by talking a little bit about how I found astrology. I did mention this a little bit yesterday on the opening panel, but I think it's so important, particularly for a conference like this. When I think of queer, I also think of "make it up as you go along," make up your own rules because no one's ever done it that way before. I'm a totally self-taught astrologer who one day found a used book at a bookstore, taught myself, got my chart online and started reading it, and I think a lot of people find astrology that way. They're initially interested to learn more about themselves, and then they start reading to see what other people in the astrological canon have written about the things in their charts.

If anyone here has ever done that, you probably encountered the same thing I encountered, which is, if you are at all *other* than what is considered to be normal or mainstream, you'll read a whole series of quite judgmental, not understanding at all, and highly pathologizing descriptions of yourself. That is what I found upon looking into my own chart. Then, of course, I started to look for where it's going to say something about how you know somebody's gay if you're looking at the chart, and I found very little reference to these sorts of things. When there was a reference, it was always these kinds of tragic stories of perverts and deviants who never found love and were abused by their parents, all of this horrific stuff...and that's a lot of what we find when we look for ourselves in mainstream astrology texts and through speakers. I think it's so important with astrology not only that we understand what's going on with the planets and the signs, but how we communicate what it is that we know.

Just an anecdotal story about my own chart: I had an astrologer look at my chart a few years ago. I have my Sun in Aquarius conjoined to Venus retrograde, and this astrologer said, "Oh! Well, there you go, you've got a Venus retrograde. No wonder you're gay, you have a problem with women!" *(Audience laughter)* Hmmm! Right? And so, like, how many things are wrong with that statement, I can't even begin. *(Audience laughter)* Suffice it to say, I don't think I have a problem with women just because I choose not to sleep with them. Venus retrograde appears in the charts of people of all different persuasions, many of whom don't have any problems with women at all.

So this is the lens through which I am approaching this topic: to make sure that we as a group are committed not to having other people who are similarly not represented in these texts hear these things. I'm confident enough to be able to say, "That's bullshit, I don't have a problem with women!" But not every client that comes to us is going to have that kind of confidence about themselves, and the way we communicate things can impact whether they're able to more freely accept who they are, or whether they leave feeling ashamed, not seen, these feelings that a lot of us have felt many times in our lives.

Jessica: Hi, I'm Jessica Lanyadoo, and I got my first astrology book when I was twelve years old. I studied it and studied it and then finally I had the opportunity when I was 17 to study it in more of a collegiate setting, and I did that for, I think two semesters, and I fell in love, and when I was nineteen I moved here to San Francisco, to become an astrologer in the Big Gay City! *(Audience laughter)*...And I definitely have, *(Laughs)* I've been doing that. *(Audience laughter)*

In '94 when I moved here, I immediately hooked up with Linea Van Horn's San Francisco Astrological Society, and I started meeting with lots of astrologers, and there weren't a lot of gay voices, and as

Barry was saying, there weren't a lot of gay texts, and for me more than that, there wasn't a lot of feminism in the texts that I was reading. So you know, once I'm already reading and talking to people and everything's "he, he, he," and I'm already decoding it into "she, she, she." And I thought, OK, I'll add on all the other things, right? Like queer, or different kinds of cultural things, that I think can be really messy and missing from traditional astrological texts.

But I've been in practice since '94, '95, and full time since '99, and I would say for at least half of that time, the majority of the people I worked with were queer, were social workers, were activists and artists, and basically "others." And that's not true anymore. I work with people across the spectrum, but what I've found is the truth tends to lie in synthesis and not in the details. And in order to synthesize information that is applicable to somebody who is queer or any kind of other, whether we're talking about gender or ability or class or race, you have to be educated and care enough to do the research and do the leg work, and you have to listen to clients and you have to listen to the news and be part of the world. As we look at and explore queer astrology now and this weekend, it's about gayness and homosexuality, but it's about so much more. It's about expanding the lens to be more inclusive and to be more comprehensive, reconnecting with a central truth, at least what I believe in my practice, that is, that astrology is about people. Ideally, it's about helping people. So if you're not connecting with people where they need help—as opposed to "that's why you have a problem with women" which is clearly not where Barry needs help. I am a woman and I love him—so that astrologer wasn't listening and was coming in with her own agenda and projecting that. And that's problematic whether we're talking about gay issues or any other issues.

Barry: Our talk is split into two main sections. First, we're going to be talking about a set of queer ethics that we can all bring to the consultations we do with charts and with clients. In the second section, we're going to be talking about specific astrological methodologies and how they might apply in certain situations.

In a lot of ways, I am speaking to an audience that is already oriented to this, or you wouldn't have found your way to this conference. But I think it's worth explicitly articulating some of the ways we can use our communications and interactions with clients actually to create space where folks can feel seen and heard for who they are. We were very leery in naming this talk that we weren't calling it "Talk about Queer Client Work" as though what we were saying today only applies to queer clients. It is the queer *lens*, or this way of articulating these values, that is the key to what we're talking about here, and these things apply beyond just people who identify as queer.

In terms of the astrological methodology, we're speaking practically because this is the work we do every day. We're not stepping back from the topic and thinking of how to "queer" astrology. This is just what we do every day because they are the people who are coming to us. That's what they need from us. We are going to discuss some nuts-and-bolts things you can look for in charts, with the caveat that, because we're working with queerness, not everyone can be described by these configurations, and that it's part of the very way these issues have been described in the past which are things I am personally rejecting. At the same time, there's a reason why astrology works: because we do see patterns where certain people have certain placements. So that section will be a discussion, as opposed to us being the experts; for example, "Anyone who has Venus square Uranus is like this." We want to encourage people to interrupt us with questions and observations. We really do want this to be interactive, and we really wanted to articulate that as the pedagogical strategy which goes along with a queer astrology–but that's already happening all weekend anyway, which is beautiful! It seems like that's what all the speakers here are doing. Of course, we will rein in any speakers if it starts to stray a little too far; we always like to be clear about that. But we really want this to be a conversation, as opposed to us being the ones who have the rules, because that's the exact thing that has been used against queers.

Jessica: I agree. And I'm a triple Capricorn, and I actually love the rules. I live with the rules, and because I know the rules I break the rules a lot. There are a lot of truisms I work with–just a little complexity to add to the conversation.

Barry: And her rules are really good rules. And queerness is not really a matter of gay and straight. There are people who only sleep with members of the opposite sex who still identify as queer. And there are people who only sleep with someone of the same sex who are maybe more homosexual than queer. When I make that distinction, I am saying it doesn't really have to do just with who they're sleeping with. It's not necessarily about who is putting what organ where, but it's also about a political bent—about whether they conform or don't conform in certain ways. Queerness is a lens through which to view these things, not just about gender or sex or what gender somebody sleeps with.

Jessica: Also something that I see a lot when I'm working with people, who live a straight life, is the issue of gender. I will address with them the complexities of gender and not allow them certain assumptions. If someone says, "Oh, I really want to get married," then I might say, "Well, why do you want to get married?" A lot of people will get stumped. I'd say 9.5 out of 10 times, people will tell me they've never been asked that question before. And that's important. Why do you want to have a kid? Why do you want to get married? Why do you want to be in a relationship? And all that's coming from a queer lens and really serves folks of all orientations to come at it with that lens. I think that even having a queer lens when talking about sex, the act of sex, is really helpful. A lot of women whom I work with who sleep with men are really demoralized when they are dating men who are bottoms—everyone know what a bottom is? In this room, everyone knows! (*Laughter*) You know, bottoms aren't going to initiate sex as much. And straight men are stereotyped to be tops. And what do you do if you're with a straight man who is a bottom? A lot of times, straight women will take that language as a gift—you know, it's great to have that queer lens, this is pre-existing language—and it's liberating for people. This is not a gay/straight thing, this is human complexity and all that it entails.

Barry: In terms of these queer ethics we are trying to articulate here, one thing I want to say right off the bat is that there is *no* definitive signature for finding a gay or transgender identity in a chart...any more than you can see race or gender in a chart. People are individuals. When we see this thing on a piece of paper with a bunch of little glyphs on it, we can't tell whether that person is gay or straight. That's very different than what I read when I first started studying astrology. There may be signatures for certain behaviors, but these are *identities* we're talking about. Identity is a cultural construct that people use to create a category around a series of behaviors they're lumping together. But it's not like people are born "gay" in that way. "Gay" is an identity that has arisen over a period, with a cultural history that created the idea of gay. It's not that men weren't sleeping with men always, or women sleeping with women, but that doesn't mean there was a coherent gay identity throughout history. Therefore, if we're dealing with something essential, archetypal, like we're doing with astrology, it trumps those identity categories.

Here's an example. I always read that a signature of being gay is you had some kind of a hard aspect from Uranus to your Venus or your Mars. I'm sure many of you heard this or read this or thought about this. Don't get me wrong, Uranus—the planet of the eccentric, the unorthodox, the liberated one—*does* seem to be a planet that is pretty clearly gay. (*Laughter*) But everyone who has those signatures doesn't sleep with a member of their same gender. And likewise, there are people who are gay whose signatures are more Saturn. Maybe you wouldn't know they are gay because they keep their cards a little closer to their chests, maybe they struggle with it...whereas the Uranus archetype is more exploding outward, more demonstrative. That's where these signatures don't work to describe an identity, but they do work to describe certain behaviors.

Jessica: And if I can just add something about inclinations. I can't count how many people I've seen with Uranus square Venus or Uranus opposing Venus, which I think is hella queer—not gay, but really queer—they try to force themselves into a straight or heteronormative box. And I think it deserves to be said that I feel that we are often driven more by survival than authenticity. If it is my survival mechanism to be accepted by my mom, and my mom is my best friend, but my mom doesn't love lesbians, then I'm not going to really go in that direction of expressing my homosexuality. That's just one example, but there are a million ways that our queerness can express itself. Maybe we don't want to be monogamous or maybe we don't want to spend that much time with the person we're dating. Uranus can do that to Venus. It has a lot to do with what we are willing to embody at times. We have to meet someone where they're at, not assuming that they're totally embodying certain aspects of their chart.

Barry: Since we've identified that queerness does not equal gay, and that queerness is more about living outside the dominant paradigm in general, someone may be heterosexual and live conventionally in a lot of ways but have a piece of themselves that doesn't fit the dominant paradigm. They still need space for that piece to be held and seen. And the goal of a session with an astrologer is we are giving clients permission to be as nonconformist as they want…and *also* as conventional as they want.

This is such an important piece, because we are the queers here and we have our own agenda, maybe of opening up the discussion of astrology to things that are nonconformist. But I don't think it serves our larger purpose then not also to hold room for people who are more conventional than we are, who do fit the dominant paradigm. I feel that part of our job as astrologers is to help people feel more comfortable with whoever they are. And therefore, when people come looking for advice on relationships—and for anyone who sees clients, you know that's probably number one—that success, for lack of a better word, in the relationship area is going to look different for an individual based on what it is they want. It's our job as astrologers to reframe the concept of being successful in this area…being able to find one's own satisfaction rather than fitting a particular goal.

Question: So is queer then defined by always being antithetical to the conventional?

Jessica: I don't think so. I don't like to define things as "anti-". I think queer encompasses gay, but is larger than gay. I think what we're speaking to is that "queer" is a word that acknowledges that there is individuation in this life and that we have the agency to embody our charts, to embody our individuality in ways that are self-appropriate. And we're saying this in a way, maybe what you're hearing, that sounds "against" something because many of us feel pressure to be what we're "supposed to be," whatever that means. And by utilizing a queer lens, we're taking away that "supposed to" and we're asking, "What is this person authentically? What is your truth?" And as long as it's not destructive to yourself or others, then we should have the freedom to embody that truth.

Barry: I think there's something that happens when we use queer as a verb and we talk about "queering" something. My first reaction to anything I'm told I'm supposed to be is to ask a question. It's not to have an answer which is opposite that, but to ask, why is it that I'm supposed to be this way? And do I authentically want to be this way, or am I doing it because there is some kind of pressure socially, politically, familially, and of course, from inside, because we internalize all of those things? To be queer is to have arrived at your identity and your decisions about what you want to do with your life, not just by having inherited this from others' expectations, but from having actively *inquired* into these matters. That is the difference.

When I say something is "straight" or "queer," it has to do with privilege. People who were born and knew they were going to be able to get married and have children and all those things—that's not about being heterosexual. That's straight. They've gone down the straight line that was all paved out for them. And there's nothing wrong with that necessarily, although my personal opinion is that you should always inquire into why you make the decisions you do. But when you are a queer person, you didn't have that luxury of just being able to follow the straight line. You *had* to have inquiry. It's like when someone who is not gay assumes that gay people have a choice in the matter, and we ask them, "Well, did you *choose* that you were going to be a man and that you were going to sleep with women?" No, you just *assumed* that's what you were going to do because that is what you felt. To me, queer is always about asking the questions…and the minute you think you've figured it out, there's a new dimension that trips you up a bit, and you ask yourself the questions again.

Jessica: I also think that when we include transgender folks in the conversation, we are looking at a population of people who are arguably the queerest of the queers. They're extremely queer. Let's say they were born female-representing, and then transition and look very queer. And then they've transitioned and they're now passing. Everybody thinks that they're male when they look at them and they're dating women still. There's a way that there is a transition of values that occurs, a transition of experience and of reaction to the world and of the world in reaction to them—and there's this questioning and acknowledgment of constantly changing and constantly growing that is a huge part of the queer experience.

Question: But there's this fascinating word you're using, which is "passing." If they've gone to the other side of transition and now they're passing, what does that mean? Are they "unqueered" because they've made themselves conventional?

Jessica: I think it's just about acknowledging that people react to us based on how we present in their eyes. It's acknowledging that we are part of a larger community. It's not just my chart; my chart is not a "go it alone ride." My chart is an interaction with everyone's chart in here and everyone in the world.

Question: We're a community that has such a rich history of passing, whether it's passing to disguise, or hide, or dressing up in drag. It's a very intriguing word for our community.

Barry: Yeah, I would agree…rather than draw any conclusion beyond it being intriguing, loaded, or complicated. Based on how I articulated the ways I see queer, if you've actually gone through the series of inquiries far enough that you've indeed transitioned the gender you're presenting to the world—even if you're passing as a man, even though you started out as a woman—you're still pretty darn queer if you've gone through that whole process. I don't think that passing means "Now I've lost my queer credentials."

But these questions won't be resolved here. And the gay marriage equality movement brings up interesting questions, too. You know, someone who passes and is transgender and chooses to marry someone of the gender other than how they are now identifying—is that a gay marriage? It could be, depending on where that person lives, their legal gender definition. Just saying that these are intriguing themes might be enough. Thanks for bringing up that point.

Question: It seems to me that there are gay people who aren't queer and lesbians who don't want to be dykes, and so I'm just wondering if queer actually encompasses gay. I don't know exactly what the graphic would be. (*Laughter*)

Jessica: I agree. That's a really important piece. Some straight folks are really queer. And some gay folks aren't especially, which is why we're using the concept of queer more as a receptor or something that encompasses gay.

Question: But then maybe queer encompasses "EVERYTHING." (*Laughter*)

Barry: It occurred to me, when you brought up the idea about trying to come up with a graphic for it, that it would always resist the graphic. That is the nature of queer, and we're seeing it play out even in this discussion, now that there's a lot of slipperiness in the language. I think that queer goes *toward* the slipperiness. It does not resist the slipperiness. It does not try to contain it. Every time we hit upon these slippages, we are doing something right.

Audience: I just wanted to point out something very interesting in the language, especially as we are excitedly using the word queer as a verb—queering—how closely related it is to the words query or querying. We're asking a question. To me that's what queerness is, if we could even try to define it for a moment, which instantly means we're probably going in the wrong direction (*Laughs*) But as we approach some sort of way of feeling comfortable with "What could queer astrology be?" I find that questioning is almost a foundation for it.

Barry: I love that point. Thank you.

Question: I wonder about the distinction between openly gay and closeted individuals. Openly gay people have accepted their identity and are living that, while closeted people turn their hatred inward and injure themselves and us in the process. And with what you were saying about not hurting other people, how do you work with people who are in the closet, knowing that the first step has to be liberation of some sort?

Jessica: I work with a lot of people who are closeted in San Francisco. I work with closeted clients and I'm just respectful of their boundaries, but also encouraging. And that is not encouraging to "go gay," but encouraging them to live in an authentic way, encouraging them to take risks, to be embodied. I think it's a mistake to try to push someone afraid of getting bad grades to go back to school or to push somebody to come out of the closet, to push someone to do something that they're not ready for. I think that we can be really respectful and be a witness to that fear because who of us in this room hasn't been helped in life by just someone taking a moment to bear witness to our pain. It's a transformational thing. I don't think it's always about counseling or pushing a person but about being a witness to their truth. Transformation happens from there.

Barry: Another way to help a client with that is to approach a session with these very ethics we are articulating now. Another one I can throw out there that would apply to what we're talking about is when you start a session, you explicitly articulate confidentiality up front. Anyone who's been through ethics trainings knows this. We know that's the right thing to do. But when you do that at the beginning of the session, you are letting the client know they may be able to talk about things here that they have some discomfort with themselves, and particularly if these are things that go against the dominant paradigm. A lot of closeted clients, and I am not going to say this is true for everyone, are in the closet because they are experiencing in their lives a perceived or real lack of validation. They may get rejected. They may be pushed out of jobs, living situations, familial situations, if they express that truth to other people. And if that's not a real threat for them, the *fear* of that can feel just as real. So, right off the bat, creating a space that says, "You can talk about whatever you want here, and we're not going to talk about it with anyone else," creates an invitation that, somewhere down the road, the client may be able to express their desire for another man.

Question: In a follow-up to that, how do you help the client maintain agency during a session?

Jessica: I also think in the beginning of a session, I encourage clients to think critically. I encourage people to take what works and reject what doesn't. Most of the time when people are consulting with an astrologer, they are in a vulnerable place. They are cracking something open and it's scary. I think being able to tell them, "I might say five things in this hour and four of them might be the rightest things you ever heard and one of them might be wrong. So think critically." We don't generally do that. We either trust someone or we don't trust someone. Encouraging people to have a more expansive view and still think critically, just that on its own, can be incredibly transformational.

Barry: I will tell clients we're dealing with a language that has symbols with different shades of meaning. I may choose to phrase something in a way that doesn't resonate with you. If that's the case, please don't pretend that it does. Let me know so I may rephrase it in a way that makes more sense with your lived experience. People don't only show up to the session with nerves, but they also show up with the expectation that we are the guru with the magic answers. That's a powerful position, and, I'm going to be really frank, it's a powerful position that many astrologers happily take. I do not happily take that position. I find it to be incredibly uncomfortable. As an astrologer and someone who owns a metaphysical shop, I have people come in all the time telling me about what the bad psychic has told them is going to happen to them.

My favorite story about this is about a friend of mine who went to a neon-sign psychic who told her that my friend would be married three times. So every time she'd meet a guy, she'd think, "Oh, I could marry him, and it would only be my first marriage." She has internalized what the psychic has told her, because the psychic has all the power, and the psychic had "seen" something that my friend didn't know about herself. Now we all know that psychics (and astrologers) have a range of intentions, from "I'm going to rob you blind and take all your money" to "I want to help you be your best self" and everything in between, some conscious and some not. But when you plant the seed of something like "I'm going to be married three times" into someone's head, you are actually, consciously or not, helping to create that very reality. Incidentally, this friend is currently in her early thirties and has already been divorced once. I'm just saying.

I invite clients to be conversational, and I let them know they are already the expert about their own lives. I'm just adding some goodies. I tell them this is a dialogue as opposed to a monologue. We've all had the clients who don't give you anything and they want you to give them everything. And I never know if they had a good reading or not because they are not letting me know. If I "proved" to them that astrology works or not, great, they can check that off the list. But if they actually want to help themselves, they have to give me something. It's a relationship. You get what you give. So I encourage clients to be an active participant in the reading, and I think humility on the part of the astrologer is one of the most important qualities to bring to the session.

Question: How are you using the term agency?

Audience: It's making sure the clients are the agents of their own lives and that they are able to act on their own behalf.

Question: Anybody who is an astrologer is aware of how unique each one of us is. And what is so fascinating about the language we are using is that we are struggling to define not only queer, but unusual, out of the ordinary, explicitly different. We get to be pioneers.

Barry: That's a great point. I wish I had faith that all astrologers were seeing things that way, but in my experience, they are not.

Jessica: People's values differ. I've been in astrological environments with other astrologers where straight men walk up to me and ask me where my Venus is. They are asking me where my Venus is so they could manipulate me or they could understand me "as a girl." And this is something that comes from their values as straight men. They were definitely not gay men. (*Laughter*) So it's about our values, and our assumed values on some level rather than our analytic values.

Audience: I didn't like the word queer, but I have a better understanding of it after attending this. The closest aspect that I have is Venus square Uranus…which you remember as the aspect most often cited as the "gay" aspect. Rather than having anything to do with sexual orientation, I can really identify this as creative and unusual and could apply to either "straight" or "gay," not one or the other. And just because a couple is gay, that doesn't mean they're queer. They could be very conventional, you know…I just appreciate you helping me understand this.

Audience: One of the most important parts of this conference is to get together as practicing astrologers, and to challenge our own lenses through which we see the world and to embody the questions. "Queering" as a verb means to me to apply the understanding of the intersection between who we are as astrologers and our clients and between authentic being and culturally defined roles. So if I say I'm practicing queer astrology, it means that I don't leave out race, gender, sexual orientation, class, gender rules, etc. I don't leave any part of the person out, or I try really hard not to. I invite that in as part of the conversation and at the same time I have to challenge my own assumptions and the lenses that I look through.

It's also important to see who astrologers are, generally speaking: white, middle class, heterosexual or straight, or of a certain experience of the world. All of that has shaped how we use astrology. We have to understand how our own experiences and values intersect with the astrology we practice.

Barry: I want to make a few more points about the ethics. One is that it is incredibly important to respect the language that clients use to describe themselves and their own experiences and whenever possible in the consulting environment, to mirror that language back to them. When we subtly change their language, it can also be an unconscious way that we are imposing our interpretive structure onto them. Likewise, we may consciously choose to *change* the language they are using to describe their experiences, as a deliberate act. But if we are going to do that, we should explain our thoughts on that matter, in order to help the client see why we are reframing their language.

Another one is not making assumptions based on their appearance as to how they identify themselves, such as who they sleep with, whether the people they sleep with are the people they form meaningful relationships with or not, whether they are more assertive or not. As Jessica taught me, in sessions with clients she asks, "Who do you sleep with: men, women, or both?" It's okay to ask these questions if they come up. We don't want to make someone uncomfortable, but if we are having a discussion and we have a question about something, we should be able to respectfully ask them a question rather than assume. I think it's far worse to have an assumption floating out there in the watery unarticulated space than to say, "I'm not clear about something." If you've already set these ethics in place from the beginning of the session, then they'll be able to tell you if they're uncomfortable going there, and, more likely than not, they want to have that conversation. That's why they've come to see you.

Jessica: Another one is not assuming relationship structures. Not assuming that people are monogamous, not assuming that people want to be in a relationship, or if they say they want to be in a relationship, not assuming that they've thought through why they want to be in a relationship. We have to be so expansive that we don't make assumptions, not even the assumptions that they want us to make. We come to astrologers and we want them to make assumptions about us to just hurry things along. (*Laughter*) But it's not a great idea. Part of why I ask every single person—no matter how flaming or conventional they seem—that question, "Do you sleep with boys or girls or both?" is because it creates normality and fluidity around these topics. Most people, of all different persuasions, will flinch when I ask them that question, and I think it's because people aren't asked that question. When we create normality or an ease or fluid energy around something that is not accepted easily in one's general community, it creates acceptance and permission. And this gives permission for them to bring up other things and issues that we may not even see.

Question: What kind of situation would necessitate that question being asked?

Jessica: For me, almost every single reading that I ever do, because the conversation goes into dating and I need to know what pronouns to use. I don't want to be disrespectful of pronouns. A lot of people will refer to "the person I'm dating" and they don't necessarily "out" the pronoun they're using.

Question: And do you ask the client as well what pronouns they prefer?

Jessica: Personally, I try to squeeze it into the question, "Do you date boys or girls or both?" If they tell me they are dating this person named Jo, I might ask them what pronouns they prefer for me to use for that person if it feel applicable. And I might ask the client to define what pronouns they prefer if it comes up in a session. I mean, we could spend 30 minutes discussing pronoun and gender, and I don't think that's why they are coming to see an astrologer.

Barry: And I think you can have an entire session without using pronouns at all. In writing weekly horoscope columns, I can write a whole article about your love life and not use any pronoun. I mean, this is an intuitive art. So if I'm in a moment and we are sharing an energy, I do feel in my heart confident about whether to broach a question like that because my main purpose in the session is to be there for them. If I focused all my psychic energy on the other person, I'm going to know if they want to be asked a question like that. If I don't, then I'm probably not a very good astrologer.

Jessica: We both use the harm-reduction model which involves accepting people where they are at. In a session, it's so important not to have assumptions or ideas about where people should be, but taking them where they are starting from, which is related to gender and sexuality and so much more. I have pretty progressive values, but when I'm in a counseling session, it's not about my values; it's not about my agenda. It's about who I am talking to, and how I reconcile that is by having a lot of space for people to be different. I've seen many times over the years in relationships I've had with clients that they would, for example, start off really angry if I talked about substance abuse, and then they ended up getting sober. So it was a helpful thing that we had this critical conversation. Or people who are closeted and then slowly come out to friends, then family, then their employer. Change happens, but you need to start with people where they're at and give them space to change at whatever pace they need or want to.

Barry: The last ethics guidelines I want to bring up has to do with being able to recognize as a practitioner your own discomfort and to do one's best not to project one's own personal values onto the client we are advising, and not to demonize other things, such as issues of class. We've brought up class a few times in this conversation, and I think there is some kind of connection between the queer impulse and having some kind of class consciousness. We have to be certain that we're not demonizing poverty, but we're also not demonizing class privilege in terms of the actual interaction with the client. I think this is a common thing that happens with those of us of a particular political bent; we often have an ideological prejudice, that you can't be a spiritual person and have a certain degree of economic privilege. We may have our own political views on things, but when we are in a session with a client, it's about the client and who they are and where they are. This also has to do with how people are in their bodies–being size-conscious, ability-conscious, trans-positive and sex-positive. It's not about what I think, but about how I help the client.

Audience: And also religion. Don't assume that just because they are coming to you for a session that they are not a conservative Christian.

Jessica: I'd like to jump into some methodology now. I think it's really easy when talking about sexuality to talk Venus/Mars. And I think there is some value to that. For me personally, I think Venus "gender," Mars "fucking." I don't see Venus as girl gender and Mars as boy gender. I think that's limited and archaic. As far as the Self goes, we are all Venus, we are all Mars and we all have agency about how we get to experience and express those impulses in our charts, and it's on a continuum. So sometimes I am wildly Martian—I bet you can't picture it! (*Laughter*)—and sometimes I am very Venusian. And I get to embody that. And we all get to choose.

Barry: One astrological note about Venus and Mars that has helped me break it out of gender: Both Venus and Mars in the traditional system have one positive sign and one negative sign in which they are dignified. They each have a *yin* expression and a *yang* expression. When you think about the elements they are dignified in, that helps me understand their expression as well. Venus is dignified in an Air sign and an Earth sign, Libra and Taurus. Air tells us how we relate to other people intellectually, socially, and Earth, the practical bonds we make to each other—speaking more metaphorically about Air and Earth. Mars is dignified in Fire and Water signs—Aries and Scorpio—it's more about these physical and emotional drives. As Jessica said, how we fuck who we fuck. Using the elements to help us understand how these planets work breaks us out of the gender thing.

Question: Do either one of you have a clue about where in the chart you would have an indicator of coming out?

Barry: Everyone comes out under different circumstances. Some people are forced out; some people have a wonderful experience; some people have a traumatic experience. And I would be more likely to see their experience of coming out based upon what's happening for them astrologically. Someone who comes out when Pluto is on their Midheaven is going to have a different experience than someone who comes out when Uranus is on their Sun. So I don't think there's a signature for that.

Jessica: I would add to that something that Ian said yesterday which is that it's not usually like "I'm out." (*Laughter*) There's usually a process of coming out, layers and levels of coming out. How you fall in love, with whom, your sexuality. Just because one's gay doesn't mean one talks about one's sexuality or who one dates with one's family or associates. There are layers of it. And also people's sexualities change and their genders change.

So back to some methodologies. We have talked about Uranus as queer. I think this isn't about gay, but about living outside of heteronormative expectations and embodying eccentricity. Looking at Uranus can be a good indicator in terms of opening up a conversation about queerness.

Neptune I often find in relation to dysmorphia, which is a warped or disconnected self-image. So the queering effects of Neptune can sometimes be associated with some people who are trans, though not necessarily. None of these are rules. The Neptune connection is for people who experience themselves differently than the way they are perceived or the way they feel they are supposed to behave. That's Neptune's function and it's important to look at.

Okay, I'm listing, you guys, but here goes. Eighth House Saturn. It would be easy to look at someone with an 8th House Saturn and say, "Well that's not a very sexual person." But that's not necessarily the case. Saturn deals with repression and constriction. So repression and constriction with sexuality could mean they're not really comfortable with sex. It could mean that they're super monogamous and they need a lot of unwinding that happens before sex. It could also mean that they're rather perverted. They may like BDSM, (bondage, domination, sadism, and masochism) stuff, maybe a lot of control issues even if it's just in their minds, or they go into a relationship where that dynamic isn't played out in the bedroom. Or if it's more integrated and conscious, it could be more twisted in the bedroom. If I see someone with Saturn in the 8th who says they have a lot of casual sex, I usually ask them how much they drink and/or party, because Saturn in the 8th House has a hard time giving it away for free when it's not drunk. Saturn in the 8th can have a hard time being embodied during sex.

Neptune in the 8th I would also say is not a casual sex dynamic. If someone with Neptune in the 5th or 8th says they want to keep it casual or go slowly, I tell them, "Do not snuggle." Because if they start snuggling, they'll fall in love with them. You have to be very careful with that. Neptune is about merging based on ideals.

Barry: We're talking about queerness, about appreciating difference. Sometimes when Neptune is in the 8th, the person doesn't want to see or admit how *different* people are from one another. Sometimes, they can omit difference because they want to maintain those Neptune feelings in their union.

Jessica: Also with Neptune in the 5th and 8th, I always look at safe sex. Neptune has a hard time with boundaries. And what is a condom? It is a boundary. The act of getting a condom out, using a condom or whatever kind of latex we may be using, it is verbalizing a boundary. It is saying, "Slow down. This is what I need. I think you're a wonderful person, but I also think I'm a wonderful person and this is the boundary I need." A lot of time people with Neptune in the 8th or the 5th aren't comfortable asserting a boundary. They forget to assert the boundary. Or they are too concerned with what the other person is experiencing or feeling, so that they think they don't have a right to assert that boundary. So safe sex is an important topic for these placements or Neptune in hard aspect to Venus or Mars as well.

And also I've found many times that there is actually a latex sensitivity for those with these Neptune signatures. The body is actually saying "no boundaries." I then encourage people to find Good Vibrations online or somewhere else to find safe sex tools and latex alternatives.

Substance use can also be associated with this as well–8th House, Neptune, and safe sex. Keep condoms everywhere–in your purse, back pocket. By checking in about this, by initiating a conversation, we might be giving people an opportunity to talk about things that they don't have a chance to talk about anywhere else. This is valuable for gay, straight, and other.

Barry: Keep going.

Jessica: All right. I'll keep going. Uranus in the 8th can do casual sex well. Uranus can hit it and quit–gay, straight or otherwise. So this is the really nice thing about Uranus. (*Laughter*) It's convenient you know, to get your needs met and not necessarily have to get married for it.

Barry: I just want to add that we're talking about the 8th House, and haven't articulated why. As I see it, when we're looking at the chart, we're looking at the 8th House for sex. But it also shows up in the 5th House, which is sex for pleasure, a little bit easier and lighter, and sex for procreation as the house of children. In the 8th House, we're doing something a little deeper, a little more complicated, potentially more intimate and potentially more risky. And it's interesting these two houses are in square to each other, which to me says that sex is a complicated topic we can't sum up with one symbol or one house.

Jessica: Also, looking at reproduction as not just a straight person issue–reproductive needs, ability, and cycles. We all have hormonal cycles. Uranus in the 5th can indicate an erratic hormonal cycle. So for women that's ovulation. That's a really important part of sexual desire, sexual drive, and the ability and drive for reproduction. I'm personally a huge fan of people who do not have the desire to procreate. I encourage them not to procreate. There's a big difference between the desire to procreate and the desire to parent. A lot of gay folks know there's a difference but a lot of straight folks don't. So applying the queer lens in that case can be really expansive for everybody.

With Pluto in the 8th House, I think it was Donna Cunningham who said that the sexual experience can feel like a light switch: It's not you, and either your passions are off or they're on. So you're in this blaring space of desire and intensity or you're in the space where you don't see anything and you feel completely disassociated from your sexuality. It's quite an intense placement. In the 8th House, we have the theme of compulsion. How does this person stay present or silently try NOT to be present? I always want to look at substance use with that as one of the many ways we have for disassociating.

In the 8th, Pluto can be pretty pervy as well. In the 5th, it's not necessarily pervy but encourages one to explore whatever it is that they like. For women of all sexualities, that often means encouraging them to explore the wide world of porn. I'm not advocating for porn or against porn. It's just encouraging people to use the resources that are out there for them to explore their sexuality, and for having a sexual experience alone. For a lot of people raised as female, they don't know that those resources exist for them.

Barry: I want to talk about the 7th House a bit in terms of relationship structures. In my client work, I have an increasing number of people, whether hetero- or homosexual, who are looking at different relationship structures such as non-monogamy or polyamory. I distinguish between them in this way: non-monogamy can be sleeping with other people, and that polyamory is more about developing multiple relationships with people that may or may not go beyond the sexual. Those are not water-tight definitions so don't jump on me for that if you are a strong believer in those things.

I find that these conversations are coming up a lot. Maybe it's because my practice is in the Bay Area, I don't know. But there is a difference between believing it is okay to choose from these different relationship structures and *feeling* it is psychologically or emotionally appropriate for you. This is a big deal. I am seeing clients who have circles of friends where everyone is super queer and sex-positive and non-monogamous and poly. But their chart is telling me they probably wouldn't feel that comfortable with it. Of course, I'm never going to approach a client in a way that is imposing my reading of the chart in a certain way. For instance, if there is something like Taurus on the 7th House with, say, a Venus or Mars in Taurus in that house. Taurus tends to be one of the more conservative signs, not speaking politically, necessarily. Or maybe a Saturn in the 7th. things that aren't about being light and fluffy with how we have relationships, but indicate wanting a long-term, stable relationship. This doesn't mean that someone with Taurus ruling the 7th House can't be in a non-monogamous situation, of course not. But it means they need to feel there's some sort of stability or loyalty going on in the relationship.

Of course, it depends on where the ruler of the 7th House is. Maybe it's Taurus on the 7th, but Venus is square Uranus (a popular placement here!). Or Venus in Gemini. Then, we're adding another dimension. Or with someone with Gemini on the Descendant, we're looking at maybe giving someone permission that all of their relationship needs may *not* be fulfilled in one person. Does that mean they're going to be sleeping with multiple people? Maybe. Maybe not. Maybe it means their partner is not also their best friend. We need to be flexible in our assessment of the individual situation.

The sign on the 7th House, the planet that rules that sign and its placement in the natal chart, and any planets in the 7th House, are all going to give us an idea about the preferences in relationship structure people may have, which, of course *we* know because we're all brilliantly queer! But it doesn't have to do with whom we are sleeping with or how we are in relationships.

Jessica: So we have five minutes left. Where do we go with five minutes?

Barry: Wherever you want.

Jessica: Okay. I like the 12th House a lot. (*Cheers from the crowd*)

Barry: We have a lot of 12th House fans out here.

Jessica: We love the 12th House because it's hard to get reliable information about the 12th House. You know, we all have an unconscious; we all have these subconscious issues. I also see the 12th House as where we can find prenatal conditions, what was going on in our parents' relationships or any of the adults around us until we are seven years old–which I think has a huge impact on what we believe to be possible in ourselves and the world. And that has everything to do with our sexuality.

When we're looking at planets in the 12th and the cusp ruler of the 12th House, we are seeing how we value our sexuality. In a way, sexuality is equally unconscious for all of us. I mean we can be totally conscious of our sexuality, but sex is also about the underbelly. In this regard, the 8th House is not the only place we can find the deep mucky internal stuff around sexuality. When we find planets in the 12th House, in particular Venus and Mars–which is our gender and sexuality stuff–we can see the ways that we attract people to express those planets for us, so it's the projected form of experiencing the planet. And that is not generally super fun for us when we're doing that. So when I see planets in the 12th House I want to ask questions about what roles the individual plays in his or her relationships. There's a way that people can't embody a planet in the 12th so they have to attract someone to do it for them.

If I may take a moment to speak to STDs, I see things in the chart that can indicate a predisposition to STDs, people who are more inclined toward risky sexual behavior or have a harder time being embodied during a sexual experience with another human. It is a rare day that I would say to a client, "Oh yeah, you probably have STDs," (*Audience laughs*) but there are ways to speak directly to that, asking about having safe sex. My experience is that with heterosexual people they will generally say yes, they are having safe sex. And then if I ask them "Are you using condoms?" they will generally say no. Don't assume safe sex means the same thing to everyone. There are hints in the 5th house as well as the 8th house and also in looking at Neptune and Pluto, as to whether people are not prioritizing self-care, not having boundaries, being risky in ways that can easily lead to STDs.

This isn't precisely astrological, but being in a queer demographic where there's so much language and process about sex, gender and roles. I am intimately familiar with the language. People who live straight lives, however, don't often have that language. You know they have girlfriends and boyfriends, husbands and wives, and SEX (*Audience laughter*). Their experience is in the dominant culture, and there's a way to bring queer language and a lack of assumptions into straight conversations, so that everybody wins. It's not about a "gay agenda." It's about leaving more space for the human experience and having more language for their experiences. As astrologers, we're in a great position to do that.

Barry: I like it.

Jessica: I do too.

Barry & Jessica: Thanks, I think we're done.

(*Loud applause*)

Queer Astrology Anthology

Ecosexuality: Liberating the Venus within Pluto.[1]

Erica Jones

I would like to begin with a poem written by the human rights activist and scholar of nonviolence, Barbara Deming, in 1940.

> Have been not admitting it all to be present, and given.
> Dreaming.
> If love, love. Possible or impossible because of other
> person. But actual, not dreamt.
> And I no more the victim of than anyone of any
> love. This is not the devil. It is the devil who
> says this is the devil.
> Will look at everything, will not turn eyes down or
> sidewise. For it is not for me to say where the hope
> lies, where death is made life.
>
> This stiff shroud of ice, this mock of bloom,
> this weight, this glittering load with the appearance
> of feather, is promise given of spring, this anything
> but green, this load from above, most icy, most harsh,
> yet there it is–spring.[2]

At my birth, the Sun, Mercury, and Neptune were gathered in council in Sagittarius, while the Moon, Pluto, and Venus communed together in Libra as Jupiter allured them from his perch in Aries. And when I was born, the human world was just awakening to the impact of

---

[1] Author's Note: I would like to acknowledge the scope remaining to include a greater diversity of cultural figures, movements and voices in this presentation. My desire to research and collect such additional astrological evidence was unfortunately eclipsed by a very challenging year—and to Uranus–Pluto, I bow.

[2] Barbara Deming, "Have been not admitting it all to be present, and given" in *I Change, I Change: Poems by Barbara Deming*, ed. Judith McDaniel (Chicago: New Victoria Publishers, 1996), 70. Reprinted with permission of Judith McDaniel.

human population and resource consumption, and the cypress swamps, turkey oak sand hills, and flatwoods of North Florida which first nurtured my soul, body, and mind had already been devastated by the short-sighted greed of a society fixed to a notion of progress harnessed to infinite industrial growth. Yet for me, a sense of belonging came not from human society but from what we call the natural world, finding my comfort and best company amidst cypress knees and cardinals, Spanish moss and gooseberry.

In the spirit of inclusion—for I riddle you all that to include is to belong—I would like to invite everyone to take just a few moments of reflection, to settle into the body and relax on your chairs, feeling the support of gravity and the Earth under you, and recall a place in the natural world which was special to you, when you were a child. For those who didn't have access to green spaces as children, try to recall any place in which you felt at ease, comforted, or a sense of joy and wonder, openness...I invite us all to spend a moment remembering these special places, conjuring them in our imaginations, with all the comforting sensations and memories they evoke.

Thank you for that. I invite you all to come back into the room and I would like to welcome the benevolent spirit of those places into the room with all of us, that all of our deep, supportive relationships be recognized and honored in this exploration together. My talk will include the familiar abstract communication of ideas—Mercury—but I also intend to invite other windows of knowing, including the somatic or bodily, the intuition, and the imagination, for all of these inform our experience of life, including astrology, and I hope we can elicit deeper knowing thereby. Perhaps each of you with astrological familiarity could even reflect on what archetypal flavor those favorite places from childhood hold for you.

I came to astrology through the work of Richard Tarnas, whose books *Cosmos and Psyche* and *The Passion of the Western Mind* have contributed significantly to my personal and intellectual journey, even bringing me here from Seattle to the California Institute of Integral Studies to study archetypal cosmology, astrology and integral ecology.

I would like to begin with one of Tarnas' ideas on the evolution of human consciousness, particularly as it pertains to the journey of the western mind and that which has built modern industrial society with its humanistic ambitions to control and bend the natural processes of Earth to its whim. Here I must underscore that I am not privileging the modern industrial development or any Western-flavored worldviews over others, nor am I making any claims of superlative worth or value over and above other worldviews and ways of interacting with Earth and cosmos. My focus on this worldview derives from the fact that this development of consciousness is what produced a scientific method and ambition which is changing the chemical composition of our oceans and of our atmosphere, driving massive extinction of life, and it is a worldview which has effectively colonized the planet—not literally, but effectively, and for these reasons, I have chosen to focus on it.

Additionally, I present this framework as a way to examine and reflect upon some of the developments of human consciousness—and not as some absolute, unalterable truth, and I don't want to suggest that with this model. I believe one of the key psycho-spiritual and political developments of our time concerns the nature of relativity and perception, and seeing through the illusion of an absolute, object reality existing outside of our interaction with it. In the worldview in which I live, knowing is endless; mystery leads. Where there is consciousness—as represented by the Sun—there is unconsciousness—as represented by the Moon. In other words, I offer this in the spirit of inquiry and reflection, rather than dogmatic certainty.

While Tarnas presents a model of the evolution of consciousness in *Cosmos and Psyche*, he has not yet published an additional overlay of planetary archetypes which I will present, which was gleaned from recordings and lecture notes from classes he gave in fall 2008[3] and fall 2010[4]. Richard Tarnas is a meticulous scholar and researcher, providing many examples from cultural history to back up his assertions, but I won't be able to cover that in too much detail as it exceeds the scope of this presentation.

Let us begin with the notion that human self-reflective consciousness has been birthed out of the matrix of a living planet in a very long process. We did not arrive on a finished and made planet, deposited as if a new addition from a factory assembly line; we are evolving—Pluto—within a conscious relational field so vast—Neptune—it is impossible to rationally comprehend. In fact, humans could be said to

---

[3] Richard Tarnas, "Freud, Nietzsche and Jung" (course, California Institute of Integral Studies, San Francisco, CA, September - November, 2008). My gratitude to Chad A. Harris for making recordings of this class available to me.
[4] Richard Tarnas, "History of Western Thought and Culture: An Archetypal Perspective" (course, California Institute of Integral Studies, San Francisco, CA, September – December 2010).

be a part of the Earth and of the cosmos which has recently become aware of itself.[5] That is to say, humans and reflexive consciousness itself are no strange aberrations in a cosmos devoid of intelligence, purpose, and meaning, but are rather a part of a greater whole which is itself intelligent, purposeful, and meaningful beyond that meaning which is constellated in relationship to the human being.

As I attempt to describe different experiences of existence, I would like to encourage everyone to engage the imagination to step inside other worldviews and also to notice any bodily sensations which arise. If it becomes uncomfortable, you might call upon the spirit of your childhood places of comfort and sustenance for some support and grounding.

Richard Tarnas proposes that the primal worldview which has been evolving since the emergence of *Homo sapiens sapiens* some 200,000 years

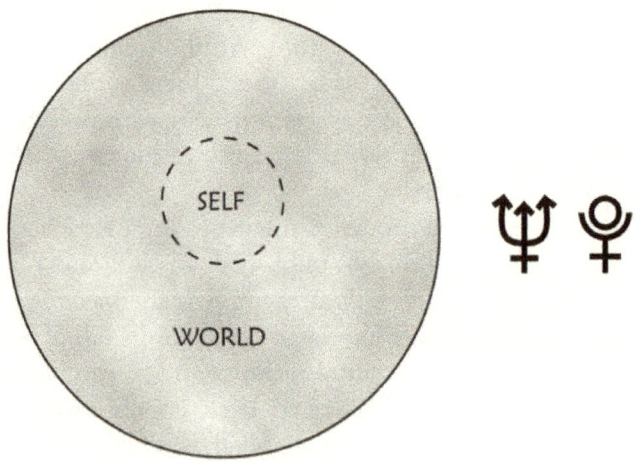

Primal World View

Figure 1. In the primal worldview, intelligence and soul (the shaded area) pervade all of nature and the cosmos, and a permeable human self directly participates in that larger matrix of meaning and purpose in which it is fully embedded.[6]

ago could be characterized in broad terms by the archetypes of Neptune and Pluto, spirit and nature, respectively, where the human being

---

[5] Brian Swimme, *The Universe is a Green Dragon: A Cosmic Creation Story* (Santa Fe, NM: Bear & Company, 1985), 58-9.
[6] Ibid., 18. Used with permission of the author.

experiences itself as an undifferentiated unity with the Earth and with all of creation. Neptune and Pluto are joined as one whole in the human being, who does not regard herself as separate from the Earth, but in unity with it.[7] Sexuality is sacred, divine, and all the world ensouled and animated with sacred meanings and purpose.[8] I must add that this experience of the Earth is still alive amongst some groups on the planet.

Then Tarnas identifies the key moment of what the German philosopher Karl Jaspers called "The Axial Age," roughly the period from 800 to 200 BCE when a great religious revolution happened across the planet within many cultures, each receiving a unique revelation or experience of a transcendent–that is, above and beyond the phenomenal world of the senses–dimension of divinity, in which the ultimate purpose and meaning and value of life was located. This transformation bears many consequences including the democratization of religion, in that different persons could claim a special connection to the divine, which was no longer the province of kings and shamans alone. Tarnas suggests that this movement is key to the emergence of the *modern* sense of the human individual.[9] Although people did experience individuality prior to this development, he argues that it wasn't the first identity a person held. The primary experience of the self had been as a member of a collective, which makes sense given the social nature of the human being and how the survival of the individual is so interdependent with the collective, a reality far more apparent in previous times than it is for many at this moment.

But this perception of a divine transcendent dimension also arrived at the cost of devaluing this world, the body, the Earth, nature and all the imperfections that accompany life. Neptune eventually becomes isolated within this outer, unearthly realm and Pluto is differentiated in a negative cast and isolated within the Earth–unclean, impure, the realm of temptation. In this movement, there is no divine in the material world, which becomes the rejected. Over time, the material world becomes feminized, whereas the transcendent is masculinized, so that Neptune is angelic, divine, the benevolent god, while Pluto is the bestial, the body, the temptress, the fallen, the messiness of biology, blood and guts, all made quite other and apart from the sacred dimensions of

---

[7] Richard Tarnas, "Freud" class lecture, October 24, 2008.
[8] Richard Tarnas, *Cosmos and Psyche: Intimations of a New World View* (New York: Viking Penguin, 2006), 16-7.
[9] Ibid., 23, 415-6.

Neptune. This world is subject to death, as Pluto, whereas the posited transcendent is eternal bliss, everlasting life, as Neptune.[10]

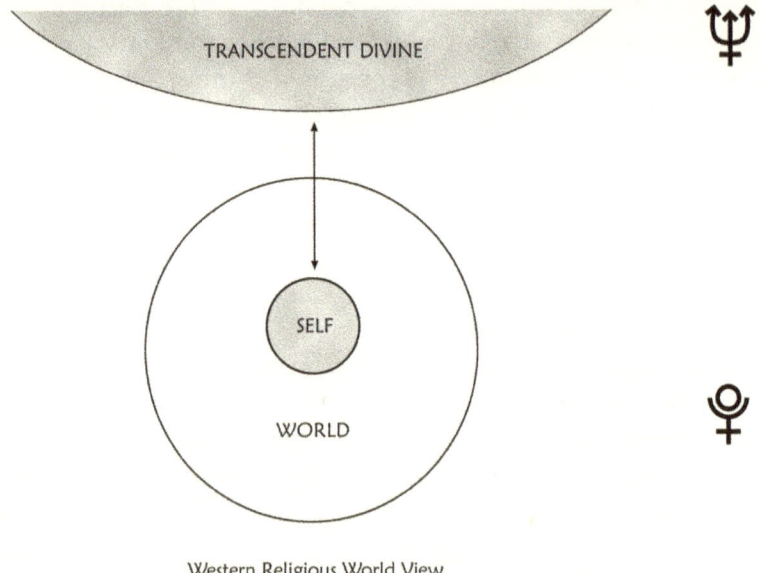

Western Religious World View

Figure 2. In the Western religious worldview that emerged between the primal and modern, forming a link between them, the human self bears a unique relationship to a transcendent divinity that is separate from and sovereign over the created world, a world perceived as increasingly devoid of meaning and purpose (represented by the shaded areas) other than that associated with the human self.[11]

This worldview is also alive on the planet today, as is the primal. In one of his 2008 lectures, Tarnas quotes Rev. Billy Graham's response to a hurricane devastating the Carolinas, in which Graham is consoling those who have lost so much: "If we don't have faith in God the father, we're at the mercy of mother nature." Graham's exhortation encapsulates the transcendent alienated from any kind of immanent divine, and how this worldview regards our mortal belonging on this planet.

A further important point which Tarnas makes here is that this begins to place all the importance upon human history as the vessel of divine purpose and meaning, placing the Earth in the backdrop as a

---

[10] Richard Tarnas, "Freud" class lecture, October 24, 2008.
[11] Ibid., 24. Used with permission of the author.

mere stage, whereas in the preceding primal view, nature is coextensive with the divine.

In this framework, a third movement which Tarnas identifies happens through the Copernican Revolution. Up until the fifteenth century in European thought, the Earth was believed to be the center of the universe until the scientists Kepler and Galileo were able to confirm Nicholas Copernicus' theory that the Sun was in fact at the center and the Earth was revolving around it as just another planet among planets. The Copernican Revolution occurs when the cosmos of the European mind is re-centered from the Earth to the Sun, and the impact of this revolution in consciousness has spread the world over via a scientific method which impacts everyone globally now, whether they are taught to believe in or practice it or not.

In any case, this is a tremendous development to which I cannot really do justice in such a short time, but for our purposes, I offer Tarnas's planetary archetypal analysis that, following on the Axial development, we experience a further splitting between Neptune and Pluto, where the Sun—as the new center of the universe—becomes identified with Neptune, and the Moon becomes identified with Pluto.

Tarnas identifies a gendered movement here, where "woman" becomes identified with the body and with nature and made to hold a very negative charge for the pure, clean, and holy male, who can only become so "pure" by using someone or something as a dumping ground for any part of him which is unwanted, in an attempt to escape this world of imperfection, taboo, temptation.[12]

A crucial consequence of the Copernican Revolution came from the experience of disproving our senses, of suddenly realizing that our senses which perceive the Sun as moving—it rises over the horizon, it sets behind the horizon—are false, and this produced a radical empowerment of human reason and eventually, in this third phase, human reason is equated as the center of the cosmos, infallible and powerful and able to illuminate everything.[13]

---

[12] Richard Tarnas, "Freud," class lecture, October 26, 2008.
[13] Richard Tarnas, *Cosmos and Psyche*, 4 – 11.

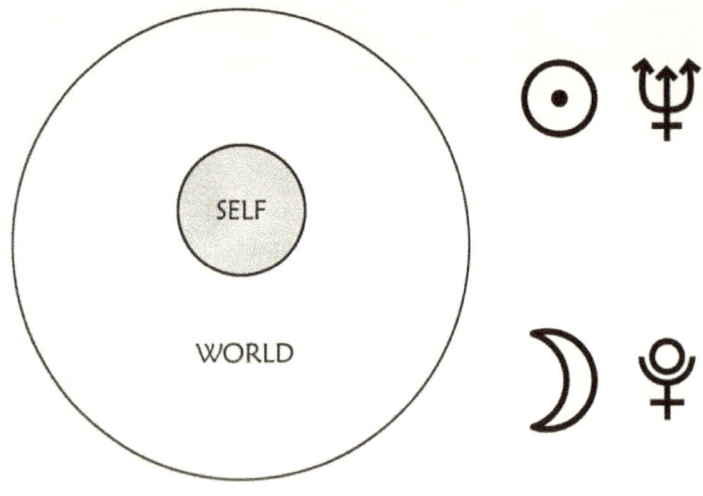

Modern World View

Figure 3. In the modern worldview, all qualities associated with purposeful intelligence and soul (represented by the shaded area) are exclusively characteristic of the human subject, which is radically distinct and different from the objective non-human world.[14]

And the sensual, the bodily, the Earthen, these are correspondingly further repressed into the shadow of the European Enlightenment as we have the French philosopher Rene Descartes' proclamation, "I think, therefore I am." Over time, all meaning and purpose becomes aggrandized to the human being, as the entire *anima mundi*, or soul of the world, is arrogated to the human. The phenomenal world becomes ever more empty of meaning, to quote Blaise Pascal writing in 1670, "The eternal silence of these infinite spaces fills me with dread."[15]

I again encourage everyone to continue to engage the imagination and notice the bodily response to what I am depicting here, what the body's intelligence might contribute to your understanding.

Tarnas depicts a fourth movement in this evolutionary development which captures the dynamics emerging in the mid-nineteenth century to the beginning of the twentieth century, wherein Darwin, Marx, Nietzsche, and Freud begin to disregard the divine altogether in their

---

[14] Ibid., 18. Used with permission of the author.
[15] As quoted in ibid., 44.

exploration of Earth, cosmos, and the human being, and we see the disenchantment of the cosmos in full bloom, as the solar logos–the mind, reason–of the Sun becomes identified with Pluto, while the Moon is paired with Neptune.[16]

Tarnas explains that because God is now effectively dead in the secularized mainstream culture, the Sun withdraws from Neptune, and nature becomes the focus of all exploration and urgently important to understand–not for its own sake of course, but for the purposes of control and prediction or dictation, quite like a ruthless Sun-Pluto. Neptune, as the spiritual or religious dimension of the human, is seen as shallow and weak, feminized and also reduced to "childlike fantasy," where the Moon symbolizes the feminine and the child. One only need contemplate this quote from Sigmund Freud, who himself is a Sun-Pluto, Moon-Neptune person,[17] "[Religion] comprises a system of wishful illusions together with a disavowal of reality, such as we find...nowhere else but...in a state of blissful hallucinatory confusion."[18]

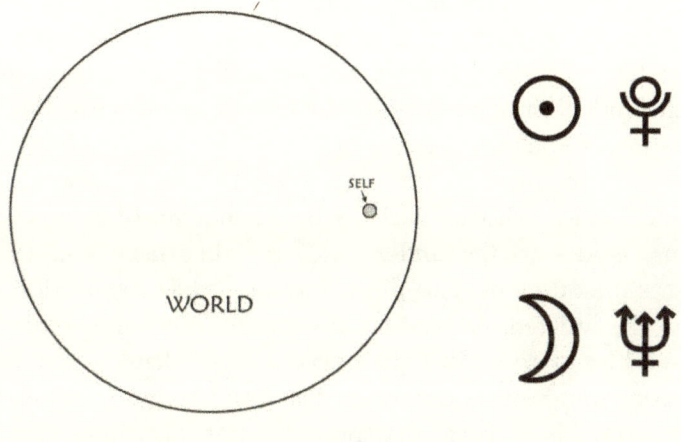

Late Modern World View

Figure 4. In the late-modern post-Copernican, post-Nietzschean cosmos, the human self exists as an infinitesimal and peripheral island of meaning and spiritual aspiration in a vast, purposeless universe signifying nothing except what the human self creates.[19]

---

[16] Richard Tarnas, "Freud," class lecture, October 26, 2008.
[17] Sigmund Freud born May 6, 1856 at 6:30 p.m. in Příbor (Freiberg in Mähren), Czech Republic, Rodden Rating: AA.
[18] Sigmund Freud, *The Future of an Illusion*, (NY: W.W. Norton & Co., 1961), 55-6.
[19] Richard Tarnas, *Cosmos and Psyche*, 34. Used with permission of the author.

And so this is the modern moment for many of us, the cultures we inhabit, and certainly the fundaments of the worldview which is driving a very destructive industrial process on our home planet. The isolated, individual self in a cosmic void, relativized into oblivion. As Pascal said, "The eternal silence of these infinite spaces terrifies me."

I think that Tarnas's framework for reflecting on the development of the consciousness which drives the industrialized worldview offers some illumination of the repression of sexuality in general, of queerness in particular and the compulsion to enforce gender conformity, since instinctual and libidinal desires and emotions are so threatening to notions of purity and innocence, divinity and sanctity. We can see the fear of the body and of death, and the alienation from the world of the senses. We see the dualism dividing sexuality from the sacred, dividing directed energies from receptive energies, and the deep need for rigid conformity to gender roles because any signal from the outside world that consensus reality actually doesn't have the cosmos pinned down and that human reason, or traditional religious conceptions don't control the cosmos, is deadly to such an inflated, self-assured belief system. The concepts are far more important than the actual phenomena of the human psyche and all of our wildness–like that of an objectified nature–represents a threat to be tamed and controlled.

But to return to those four so-called "god killers"–Darwin, Marx, Nietzsche, and Freud–(who are perhaps better thought of as precursory psychopomps, guides to the underworld, for they have also led the charge into the unconscious, into the unknown)[20] they are also leading a descent from the inflated, rational mind into the uncertainty of what is not known–and let us recall that the unconscious is hard to talk about, because it's something one is not aware of! Rendering the unconscious into consciousness is a discovery process, but how, oh how one inquires–this is critical. I note that, if we agree that solar consciousness–the conscious sense of self, centering on a sense of "I am," which draws one's future towards oneself–is in fact in a Sun-Pluto moment, it is one in which the Sun is identified with Pluto, as opposed to in a relationship with it, because I am not hearing very much from mainstream industrialized culture about surrendering to the whole, whereas I do witness the drive to continue domination, to continue the patriarchal conquest of everything deemed "other" in service of prediction and control.

---

[20] Richard Tarnas, "Freud," class lecture, October 26, 2008.

Only from the margins of industrialized societies do I hear the call for a tender identification of affiliation with the Other in all its guises, which allows for the autonomous will, purpose and meaning of the Other. The Moon is still quite repressed, vilified, exoticized, demonized, as all which is considered nurturing or protective is deemed a lesser thing, a weakness of little value or simply marginal in the brutally competitive struggle to survive, which exemplifies capitalism through and through. It's hard not to see the Sun-Neptune and Moon-Pluto pairing still strongly in action, with the continued idealization of the solar masculine heroic consciousness, the power of reason to "keep us safe from nature," and from human nature, I might add.

The continued separation of the Moon from the Sun is the main point, I suppose, and we could identify many pairings to help illuminate both the karma and the dharma inherent in our contemporary drama of the evolution of consciousness. With the continued repression of the so-called feminine qualities which have been relegated to the Moon, Venus, asteroids and other astrological bodies, our relational patterns will continue in an abusive mode which is ultimately self-destructive–for as Neptune prays every day, as the Moon demonstrates to us by sheer virtue of the presence of the body, we are not alienated from the Other.

Our bodies are permeable membranes to our environment; for example, bacteria cells outnumber human cells by ten to one in the average healthy adult.[21] Our bodies are constantly regenerating such that we have a new epidermis every two weeks and an adult human liver may turn over in as few as 300 days,[22] and not through some isolated, self-contained process, but in deep communion with our environment, with our larger body, the planet Earth. Take a moment to consider the millennia-long process of glaciation which produced the topsoil that humans take quite for granted in agriculture. I could go for hours describing how the body of the Earth constitutes the human body. And this indicates the mother aspect of the planet, the Moon symbolic of two-in-oneness, as the way humans are born out of the body of another, out of the union of two different gametes, or the way in which the human species is born out of the womb of the Earth.

---

[21] Melinda Wenner, "Humans Carry More Bacterial Cells Than Human Ones," *Scientific American*, November 30, 2007,
http://www.scientificamerican.com/article.cfm?id=strange-but-true-humans-carry-more-bacterial-cells-than-human-ones.
[22] Nicholas Wade, "Your Body Is Younger Than You Think," *The New York Times*, August 2, 2005, http://www.nytimes.com/2005/08/02/science/02cell.html.

Where does ecosexuality enter into this? What is ecosexuality? One may find many definitions of ecosexuality, from sex-positive advocacy of eco-friendly ways to give and receive pleasure, as in durable sex toys, nontoxic lubricants and such; to having sex with nature actually through erotic intimacy with the waters, sunshine, winds, and natural sex toys; to the radical idea that "sex is completely natural and that all orientations and preferences" within consensual boundaries "are valid and part of the vast erotic landscape of the complex human being."[23] I am personally sympathetic to all of these approaches, and yet I would like to place a larger frame on the concept, through reference to this process of the evolution of consciousness which Richard Tarnas has articulated, as well as the dire situation on our home planet today.

Through my study of integral ecology,[24] I have come to the understanding that we humans need to return to the body in all its guises, whether personal or political or ecological; a return to and a revalorization of our capacity to feel, to emote, to give and receive pleasure. The body of which I speak is not an idealized construct that culture and tradition may dictate as "reality" (e.g., this is what a man is, this is what a woman is). These are our only forms of political and economic engagement, the Earth only exists to serve the needs my culture dictates. Pre-existing concepts are not the living bodies which will awaken us to our belonging on this planet, but rather a process of surrendering in the phenomenological understanding that our concepts are not reality, so that we aren't just rediscovering who and what a human being is, but we are making a whole new discovery!

And so the struggle for queer inclusion in the family of society seems to me akin to the struggle for the modern human being itself to return to the family of the Earth Community,[25] to break out of the conceptual trance of who and what a human being is and expand our love and inclusion, expand our sense of who is worthy of love, because queer liberation demands the acceptance of the diverse range of human emotional expression, feeling, pleasuring and relating. It is a demand to

---

[23] "What is Ecosexuality?" EcoSex Symposium 2012, accessed November 12, 2013, http://www.ecosex.org/what-is-ecosex.html.

[24] In the broadest sense, I define an integral approach to ecology as one which takes the sentient dimensions of existence into account.

[25] Earth Community is a term which emerges from the Earth Charter, a declaration of mutual responsibility to one another and the Earth, which was developed through a richly diverse and collaborative international, multiyear process. http://www.earthcharter.org/.

value and respect wild and free bodies which don't conform to social constructs. It is the affirmation of each unique expression of the love of the cosmos itself, something which seems central to me in the transition away from life-destroying, empire-based relationships towards developing generative, life-affirming Earth Community. To establish rapport with the greater Earth Community means allowing the self-determination of all organisms, which will always defy our concepts about them. Queer liberation ultimately is part of a larger quest to become more fully human. It is remembering who we are—our cosmic identity, our Earth identity.

Furthermore, the various social movements to liberate queer love, to declare it as natural and normal and divine as any other, are a great step towards the ability to enlarge a whole society's moral consideration of and moral concern with the fate of the greater-than-human world. On the one hand, to break with social norms requires individuals coming into community, going against the grain in the name of loving and knowing for oneself, outside of any cultural construct, what is right, what is good and what is true. The poet David Whyte urges us, "Hold to the truth you make every day with your own body, don't turn your face away."[26]

I hear heroism in these actions, the ability to stand in one's center and find allies to support and faithfully mirror back true beauty, and yet there is another piece to the expansion of moral concern. I also recognize that just knowing one's own self, the continuing struggle to embrace one's own self, one's own being in the face of cultural shaming and taboo requires one to be deeply receptive of one's own true self, to be tenderly open, listening to that deep "truth at the center of the image you were born with," to quote David Whyte again.[27] This is part of the process of becoming more fully human by cultivating a crucial sensitivity which, by bringing us into deeper relationship to self, brings the capacity and potential for deeper relations with the whole. I believe the human species is in dire need of overcoming these dualities and the insensitivity not only to the world, but to their own knowledge of that world, and thus themselves. Queer liberation should embolden others in society to know Self and Other in deeper ways; to open their hearts to the multitudes of expressions of love, caring, and compassion--to crack

---

[26] David Whyte, "All the True Vows," in *The House of Belonging* (Langley, WA: Many Rivers Press, 2006), 24.
[27] Ibid.

through the repression that holds us all back from connection, interrelatedness, love, and respect.

And what great discovery then awaits all who cultivate such sensitivity and presence to Self and to Other, that it is not just the human being who is individual and has an inherent meaning, purpose, and value beyond that which any human culture may assign to it–ALL beings are individual in their own way, all beings deserve to be accorded respect, and to be listened to with caring, loving attention. All beings deserve to be included for the creation of a mutually enhancing Earth Community in which we negotiate conflict through the celebration of life and our interconnectedness.

To quote ecosex activist Elizabeth M. Stephens, "We're changing the metaphor from 'Earth as Mother' to 'Earth as Lover.'"[28] I still see and honor the Earth in her mother aspect, and I would argue that owing humanity's technological advances and the adolescent way in which this incredible power is wielded–as if mommy is an infinite resource to be plundered and exploited as we please without consequence–it is imperative to begin to regard this planet as our lover. The cosmologist Brian Swimme asserts that human beings have become a geological force on the planet Earth today,[29] and as such, we need to grow into that realization and begin to care for the planet from a much more adult view, cultivating arts of loving and caring for our planet as we would a beloved.[30]

And for me, this is at the heart of ecosexuality, and something which astrology has blessed my life with, inspiring me to be good to

---

[28] Elizabeth M. Stephens, SexEcology.org, accessed November 12, 2013, http://sexecology.org/.

[29] Brian Swimme and Mary Evelyn Tucker, *Journey of the Universe* (New Haven: Yale University Press, 2011), 102.

[30] See Serena Anderlini-D'Onofrio, *Gaia and the New Politics of Love: Notes for a Poly Planet* (Berkeley: North Atlantic Books, 2009). Anderlini-D'Onofrio depicts the arts of loving as a subset of the arts of healing, the practice of which will "turn scarcity into abundance, fear into hope, hatred into love," for the arts of loving allow "emotional resources to multiply and become abundant on a planetary scale" (xvi). Through learning and practicing these deeply embodied arts, Anderlini-D'Onofrio foresees a world in which we come to trust in oxytocin, the neurochemical of love, calm and connectedness, at least as much as we trust in vasopressin, the neurochemical of fear and defensiveness responsible for the fight-or-flight response. Though I had not read this book by the time of this presentation, I was later pleased to find similar arguments for the positive contributions to ecological transformation represented by non-normative or queer sexual and erotic expression.

people and to the world, to be generous and loving: There is intelligence in the Other and it is inherent in the cosmos. There are multiple intelligences. All behaviors require intelligence; even the worst still require intelligence. I can converse with this intelligence, activate it, hopefully collaborate with it, and no more is it the domain of philosophers. It is a rising imperative for all people as our technological capacities force another look at life before we quite unconsciously choose extinction.

We are all animals, too, to invoke Pluto's intelligence. We have these soft, animal bodies which have been demonized, medicalized, and feared in various ways, and when I think of all the denial of Pluto—oh, I don't like Pluto!—I should weep for the consequences because it is a simple denial of a reality that we all have to live with. Our animal bodies are vulnerable, sensitive, soft and receptive openings to their environments, in order to receive and give love; to receive and give nourishment; to receive and give information. I believe that a return to more instinctual knowing can help to break through all the rationalization that goes into maintaining a civilization that destroys its own life support systems and help us access an ancient wisdom necessary to form an adequate response to our times.

For example, it is astounding that this culture finds the body and its digestive processes so detestable that it converts fertilizer—human manure and urine, very much Pluto's province—into poison, polluting precious fresh water and all in the name of hygiene and sanitation, which are important, because pathogens exist—but do we *deny* that they should exist? And fearing rather than respecting their existence, we should despoil the planet, deplete the soils and thereby harm our own species?[31] With a different approach to the idea of sanitation, which loves the body and accepts its products into the natural cycle of life, cities could actually replenish our extremely depleted agricultural soils. This culture could begin to love the body of the Earth. It could begin to liberate the Venus within Pluto.

And of course, from Pluto's intelligence emerges the untamable, wild nature of the human being, who will always be instinctual, and subject to breaking taboos. I am here to challenge taboos and how we hold them, but there will always *be* taboos, and I am sure most of us here

---

[31] See Joseph C. Jenkins *The Humanure Handbook: A Guide to Composting Human Manure, 3rd Ed.* (Grove City, PA: Joseph Jenkins, Inc., 2005). Also online at http://humanurehandbook.com/.

are happy to denounce murder, child and elder abuse, and all manner of violence and coercion. Yet these mistakes happen, genuinely harmful acts occur, and how are we to react? Building a prison industrial complex so that well over two million people are imprisoned, as in the United States at the end of 2011?[32] Or could we not work towards a justice that is restorative of our relations, placing victims' needs in the center so that justice is a process built within communities rather than a contract between the state and the perpetrator, so that we can work for reciprocity and build a beloved community. Again, Venus need not be estranged from Pluto.

Let us include the Earth in our beloved community by accepting that Pluto's intelligence expressed in Earth processes operates on a level beyond human concerns, as when the planet itself decides it has other things to do than preserve very unwise building on coastlines. How are we to respond? With more demands for control and new ways of mechanizing life, again, presumably for our own safety, as if humans alone animate this planet? I would suggest that this approach is not going to alleviate our problems in the long term, and that a recovery of the lunar dimension—the body—is not a heroic journey, but rather an act of surrender in service of a deeper communion, of being able to listen, attentive to the Earth, to be transformed and allow that we humans belong in a community of life; we do not own it.

Just as with Earthen bodies, the planetary archetypes interpenetrate one another; they, too, are permeable and co-constitute one another, and to liberate the Venus within Pluto—to live in cognizance of our relationship to Earth, to the Other, however difficult or painful it might also be, is to recognize the multiple intelligences, the multiple meanings and purposes, the ever-evolving and changeable nature of existence. To reach the maturation point of inclusion as belonging will serve the ends of justice which to me is a process described by reciprocity and by love itself, very much in the sense in which Cornel West declares that "Justice is what love looks like in public."[33]

And so that concludes the more Mercurial, spoken part of this presentation, and in honor of all I have said, I would like to first invite in

---

[32] U.S. Department of Justice, Bureau of Justice Statistics, *Correctional Populations in the United States, 2011*, by Lauren E. Glaze and Erika Parks, NCJ 239972 (Washington, D.C.: United States Government Printing Office, 2012), 3.
[33] Cornel West and Belvie Rooks, "ConverZations That Matter, with Cornel West," (dialogue, California Institute of Integral Studies Public Programs, San Francisco, CA, September 30, 2010).

the imagination of the planets with a little invocation and then we'll engage in an experiential remembrance of ourselves embedded in the fabric of life, our kinship with Earth's many life forms and the archetypes which animate our being.

>Hot molten Sun of the heart radiating
>its light to make day of night
>bright and penetrating illumination
>holds promise of the dark
>shadowy places where lurks
>the Moon exposing all our relations
>to the stars burning within
>a web of connection which
>may surprise us all by suggesting
>that the planets aren't separate
>out there
>revolving around the Sun
>and we here on Earth mere inhabitants
>severed by distance
>rather discovering the planetary
>bodies coextensive
>with our own
>somehow enthroned as the mind
>the psyche
>Uranus IS me, a part of my body
>a part of my soul
>we're spiraling through space
>centering together
>with Jupiter
>interpenetrating
>Saturn
>supporting
>Venus
>melting
>Neptune
>into
>Pluto, too
>the weaving of
>Chiron's compassion
>through

Mercury's information
motivating
Mars patrolling the boundaries between us
And all these planetary energies
a source of inspiration
for divinity's play
of life and death
birthing anew
asking for our opening
asking for our reception
only needing to be honored
and so included
we humans may find that we, too, belong[34]

---

[34] The original presentation concluded with a group exercise developed by Joanna Macy called The Evolutionary Gifts of the Animals, found in her book *Coming Back to Life*.

Joanna Macy and Molly Young Brown, *Coming Back to Life: Practices to Reconnect Our Lives, Our World*, (Gabriola Island, BC: New Society Publishers, 1998), 152 – 4.

References

Anderlini-D'Onofrio, S. (2009). *Gaia and the New Politics of Love: Notes for a Poly Planet*. Berkeley: North Atlantic Books.

Deming, B. (1996). "Have been not admitting it all to be present, and given." *I Change, I Change: Poems by Barbara Deming*. Edited by Judith McDaniel. Chicago: New Victoria Publishers.

EcoSex Symposium. "What is Ecosexuality?" EcoSex Symposium 2012. http://www.ecosex.org/what-is-ecosex.html. Accessed November 12, 2013.

Freud, S. (1961). *The Future of an Illusion*. New York: W.W. Norton & Co.

Macy, J. and Brown, M. Y. (1998). *Coming Back to Life: Practices to Reconnect Our Lives, Our World*. Gabriola Island, BC: New Society Publishers.

Stephens, E. M. SexEcology.org. http://sexecology.org. Accessed November 12, 2013.

Swimme, B. and Tucker. M. E. (2011). *Journey of the Universe*. New Haven: Yale University Press.

Swimme, B. (1985). *The Universe is a Green Dragon: A Cosmic Creation Story*. Santa Fe, NM: Bear & Company.

Tarnas, R. (2006). *Cosmos and Psyche: Intimations of a New World View*. New York: Viking Penguin.

—. "Freud, Nietzsche and Jung." (November, 2008). Course, California Institute of Integral Studies. San Francisco, CA, September.

—. "History of Western Thought and Culture: An Archetypal Perspective." (September-December 2010). Course, California Institute of Integral Studies. San Francisco, CA.

Glaze, L. E., and Parks, E. (2012). *Correctional Populations in the United States, 2011*. U.S. Department of Justice, Bureau of Justice Statistics. NCJ 239972. Washington, DC: United States Government Printing Office.

Wade, N. (August 2, 2005). "Your Body Is Younger Than You Think." *The New York Times*.
http://www.nytimes.com/2005/08/02/science/02cell.html.

Wenner, M. (November 30, 2007). "Humans Carry More Bacterial Cells Than Human Ones." *Scientific American*. http://www.scientificamerican.com/article.cfm?id=strange-but-true-humans-carry-more-bacterial-cells-than-human-ones.

West, C. and Rooks, B. (September 30, 2010). "ConverZations That Matter, with Cornel West." Dialogue, California Institute of Integral Studies Public Programs. San Francisco, CA.

Whyte, D. (2006). "All the True Vows." In *The House of Belonging*. Langley, WA: Many Rivers Press.

Contributors

Erica Jones, M.A., Integral Ecology, has been a participant-observer in astrology since 2006, studying principally with Richard Tarnas at CIIS. While composing a biography of Mount Diablo, a nearby mountain in Contra Costa County, Erica is also developing a community astrology model together with an astrologers' collective, all of which seek to make a transformative worldview more accessible to a wider audience. Her astrological practice is informed by ecological awareness, incorporating nature-based practices for self-exploration and reconnection to the greater-than-human world. Prevailing obsessions include the nature of causality and the revalorization of the planetary archetype Neptune (publication forthcoming).

Jessica Lanyadoo is an internationally respected Astrologer and Psychic Medium and has been in private practice since 1995. She offers sessions for couples and individuals by phone or in person and teaches small groups in her San Francisco office. Subscribe to her free weekly column, Psychic Dream Astrology, at lovelanyadoo.com.

Barry Perlman is an intuitive astrologer who's been counseling clients worldwide for over a decade. Since 2002, he's shared his astrological wisdom on his website astrobarry.com, where thousands of visitors enjoy his weekly "horoscopes that keep it real" and other writings. He is also co-owner of The Sacred Well, a metaphysical shop in Oakland, CA.

Christopher Renstrom is the creator of Rulingplanets.com, a subscription-based interactive astrology website adapted from his bestselling book *Ruling Planets* published by HarperCollins in 2002. Christopher also writes the daily horoscopes for The San Francisco Chronicle and SFGate.com. He created and wrote the horoscope column for ALLURE magazine from 1991 through 2009. Now the exclusive astrologer for Patti Stanger, The Millionaire Matchmaker, his weekly forecasts appear on Sheknows.com. Christopher was voted Best Astrologer by Utah's City Weekly in 2012 and 2013.

Ian Waisler first encountered the living sky as a youth, entranced by the moonlit sky and its unique way of speaking to him. He's been engaged in astrological study his whole life, locating it among astronomy, mythology, linguistics, ritual, and yoga. He studied with Risa D'Angeles, Jessica Murray, and Lynn Bell, in addition to completing the foundation year of the Faculty of Astrological Studies. Highly Uranian, he concedes the formality of established credentials are ill aligned with his dharma. In his dedicated study of Yoga, he continues to explore how astrological symbols live in the body, and how we can align ourselves with an illumined fullness. He's thrilled to be organizing community through this queer astrology project. Find his schedule at ianwaisler.com.

Rhea Wolf is a feminist witch and astrologer living in Portland, Ore. Her genuine desire is to help people awaken their inherent creativity, activate their authentic selves and deepen their connections to the larger world. Rhea is motivated by a vision of an emerging culture based on respect, beauty, justice, and relatedness. She is the author of *The Light That Changes: The Moon in Astrology, Stories and Time* and the *Which is Witch* zines. Her articles have appeared in "The Mountain Astrologer" and she writes the astrology column for "Hip Mama Magazine." Find her at RheaWolf.com.

Conference Contributors

Yolo Akili has worked as an astrologer and emotional wellness counselor for marginalized youth and men for almost a decade. Akili's writings have appeared in many publications including the Huffington Post, The Good Men Project and Voice Male. He has appeared on Huffington Post Live! and The Derek & Romaine Show (Sirius 1080 XM). Akili has also delivered keynotes and presentations at Vanderbilt University, Columbia University, Fordham University and much more.

Diego Fitzgerald got turned on to the art of stargazing after retiring as a professional cook. He is blessed to pursue his passion of counsel and astrology through higher education and mentorship. Over the past five years he has been working in Tibetan spice medicine under Chef Viday Bikram, cultivating a QPOC healing collective for the Pacific Northwest, and working hard at being a college boy as a student of POC lineage to better understand what we need for physical and spiritual nourishment.

Astrology has provided a space for understanding, transformation, and healing. It illustrates our unique challenges, natural talents, and reminds us that, despite the oppressive systems that be, we have a place in this universe as a part of the human experience and offers tools to heal present and ancestral trauma in ourselves.

Laurence Jones has been aware of astrology since his grandmother wished he was born 3 weeks later so he could be a Cancer. He thanks his lucky mutable stars she didn't get her wish. Through analyzing and challenging perceived gender roles and stereotypes he's looking to remove negative associations he's learned through the binary nature of mainstream astrology. You can locate his burgeoning musings on various places on the internet while he cultivates more thoughts and musings. You can find him blogging about Soul Music, Vintage Automobiles and general ephemera as well.

Lilia Leshan, MFT is a queer femme psychotherapist, astrologer, tarot reader, and performing artist. She earned her BA from Mills College in Gender Studies and Performance and her MA from CIIS in Counseling Psychology with an emphasis in Drama Therapy. She also studied opera singing at Mannes College of Music in NYC and physical theatre with foolsFury and the SITI company. In her private psychotherapy practice in San Francisco, she specializes in working with sexual outsiders, relationships, intimacy and sexuality, gender, creativity, and spirituality.

Chani Nicholas is a full time astrologer, writer and yoga teacher based out of San Francisco and LA. She holds a BA in Integral Studies from CIIS, an Associate Degree in Feminist Counseling and she is a certified Yoga Therapist and Reiki practitioner. All of her work is rooted in a queer, feminist framework and she believes that within this context the practice and application of astrology can be deeply liberating and healing. You can read her astrological musings and horoscopes at chaninicholas.com.

Rod O'Neal is adjunct professor in the Philosophy, Cosmology, and Consciousness program at the California Institute of Integral Studies (CIIS), San Francisco. He was a founding coeditor of the Archai journal and holds degrees from Vassar College (B.A., highest honors, biochemistry), UC Berkeley (M.A., biochemistry), and the California Institute of Integral Studies (Ph.D., Philosophy and Religion). His doctoral dissertation, "Seasons of Grace: An Archetypal History of New England Puritanism," is a detailed case study of the archetypal correlations between the phenomena of a particular historical movement and the outer-planetary cycles, as well as a theoretical exploration of the ancient philosophical roots of astrology and their implications for the current world view. Rod has been a professional astrologer for fifteen years, and has been involved in Western esoteric studies for nearly thirty.

Stella the Good Witch helps healers, activists and artists (and often folks who are all three) take better care of themselves so our care takers and change makers can keep doing their good work. Her spiritual practice is deeply rooted in anti-oppression work and the environmental justice movement. She was raised by witches and born on Halloween. She jokes that with a name like Stella, which means stars, being an astrologer just made sense! She's been working with the asteroids since the inception of her practice and finds that they are the crucial piece to undoing the astrological patriarchy as much as we can in the world we have.

Luciano Sagastume is a second generation Guatemalan, working as an astrologer, writer, and co-op member in San Francisco. He draws inspiration from social justice and anti-oppression work, queer theory, and Mayan time-keeping. He believes the path to transformation is through radical acceptance of the present moment, and all the ways that it may change.

For audio of all lectures given at the conference
and for more information about future conferences, please visit

queerastrology.com

www.ingramcontent.com/pod-product-compliance
Lightning Source LLC
Chambersburg PA
CBHW020912090426
42736CB00008B/594